THE SELLER'S JOURNEY

THE
SELLER'S

Your Guidebook
to Closing More
Deals with
N.E.A.T. Selling

JOURNEY

RICHARD HARRIS

PAGE TWO

N.E.A.T. Selling is a registered trademark of
The Harris Consulting Group. All rights reserved.

Cataloguing in publication information is
available from Library and Archives Canada.
ISBN 978-1-77458-406-4 (paperback)
ISBN 978-1-77458-407-1 (ebook)

Page Two
pagetwo.com

Edited by James Harbeck
Copyedited by David Marsh
Cover, interior design, and illustrations
by Cameron McKague

theharrisconsultinggroup.com

Yes, I'm in Sales

MY EMAIL IS RICHARD@RHARRIS415.COM. More on this later.

Sometimes sales kinda sucks. And I don't just mean the hard parts of winning and losing deals. Sometimes it sucks simply because those who have never done it don't know how to respond when they hear this is our career.

Heck, sometimes when salespeople tell others they are in sales you can hear the other person's voice change, and their eyes quickly look away. Almost as if in shame. Doctors and lawyers frame their diplomas and put them on their walls. We don't.

Most of us don't even have a degree in sales. Out of the approximately 4,360 higher education institutions in the US—2,832 four-year colleges and 1,582 two-year colleges—we found one source from 2018 that says only around 120 offer a degree in sales.

Here's the good part: you do not need a college degree in sales to be great at sales. In fact, you don't need a degree in *anything* to be great in sales. I would even say that you do not need a degree to be great at sales *leadership*. You may need to work on your math skills, but that does not mean you need a degree. Don't let anyone ever tell you otherwise.

And for those of us who do have college degrees, I'd be willing to bet that a huge percentage do not even have a business-related major. And I will go out even further on a limb and say a majority of us in sales never even considered sales as a career choice. We "fell into it." Which makes it sound like some kind of black hole.

Well, I am here to say stop that fucking nonsense, own yourself, and be proud to say, "Yes, I'm in sales."

One of the biggest ironies in sales was shared with me recently. I will paraphrase.

In sales, we are taught to be the agents of change, and it's our job to get our customers to embrace the change because it will be better than the status quo.

Yet when it comes to changing ourselves as salespeople, we often know we can do better and be better, but we resist changing ourselves probably more than our customers resist.

This book is written for those wanting to get better.

Maybe you are a sales rep at a horrible organization where leadership is dumb enough to think that one-on-one meetings are supposed to be all about sales pipelines. Or maybe leadership is too busy yelling "*Steak knives!*" to realize they have created a soulless culture because they want to tell their war stories about the time back in 2001 during the first dot-bomb. And deep in your gut you know there is a better way and you finally realize you have to care more about your career, because they will not—to them, your only value is your most recent revenue number.

Or maybe you're a leader looking to figure something out. Find something new that is helpful and healthy. Something that will give you and your team the specific mindset and skills necessary to sell in the twenty-first century.

Everything you read in this book comes from real-world experiences, has been tried, and is still used daily. But it's not some magic pill. You will have to adjust your mindset. You will have to challenge yourself to do something different. You will have to turn off your internal "excuse factory."

Either you are willing to do these things or you are not. And no, trying something one or two times will not be enough. Rarely can anyone hit a curveball after getting instruction and then taking two practice pitches.

If you are unwilling to make yourself uncomfortable to become more comfortable, go ahead and stop reading and get your money back. Heck, you have my email address. I can't be any more human than that, can I?

But if you want to be proud of what you do, if you want to say "Yes, I'm in sales, and I strive to be great at it," then let's go on this journey.

{ 1 }

Get Your Map and Your Compass

I'M SORRY TO REPORT that you've been lied to all through your sales career. There is no such thing as a Buyer's Journey.

Even I perpetuated this lie as a sales leader for a long time too. But the Buyer's Journey just doesn't exist. There's only a *Seller's* Journey. Everything else is about the Buyer's *Experience*.

Now, before you start yelling at me through this book or audiobook, or throwing your Kindle or iPad, hear me out for just a few minutes. (And remember, you have my email; send me your Venmo.)

Think about when you go to a restaurant. No one ever asks you, "How was your journey to the restaurant?" Nobody asks about your Uber ride or your drive there. They ask you how your *experience* was when you got there. How was the food? Was the service good? What was the ambience like? They want to know about the experience of being at that restaurant.

When we need to find an electrician, want to buy a new TV or car, or whatever it may be, we often seek advice from friends. We want to find a trusted source. If you've ever had a friend tell you not to hire a certain person or service, was it because they had a bad Buyer's Journey? No. It's because they had a bad Buyer's Experience.

Think about shopping online. We want to know what other people's experience was like, so we typically look for overall star ratings to give us a simple starting point, then we sort through the results. In my case, I love to sort the ratings from worst to best. Why? Because I want to know the worst thing that can happen. We *love* hearing about someone else's miserable *experience* so we can avoid it ourselves. Plus, it helps us remember times we've made a bad purchasing decision and feel better because we know we're not alone. In some cases, we'll ignore negative reviews because the overwhelmingly positive reviews outweigh them, and in others we'll use the negative reviews to help us choose or push us into something else.

If you're a sales leader, you know how important reviews are for your business. How often do you ask for a referral from your customers? Do you go to review sites like G2? This is where your *Buyer's Experience* shows through.

One person asked me a while ago, "What about at the very beginning, when someone decides they want to consider a purchase. Isn't that part of a Buyer's Journey?" I simply responded, "Not really, because there was some *experience* prior to that decision that made them curious."

So repeat after me: there is no such thing as the Buyer's Journey; it's all about the Buyer's Experience. All that really matters is how the Seller's Journey guides the Buyer's Experience. And we want to ensure the Seller's Journey is as impactful and positive as possible for everyone involved.

How Has Your Journey Been So Far?

I know: the Seller's Journey is *not* always as impactful and positive as possible.

Sales can be cutthroat. It can be demoralizing. And it can fuck with your mind, which then fucks with your life. And every time you get a new sales leader, they just make it worse because they think their way is the only way. And all of this can fuck with the Buyer's Experience.

Sales is fraught with differing methodologies, ideologies, opinions, mindsets, and practices. It can be really confusing. And the one thing that's missing regularly is the most important part: humanity.

So let's define humanity in sales. From our vantage point this means treating people like people first, not a number. That does not mean the number doesn't matter; it does mean the number is not the only thing that matters.

Let's take it a step further. Humanity means being humane. And simply put, if you would not talk to a child in the aggressive manner you think you can talk to a salesperson in, well, then in fact you are not being humane.

Humanity means you can be vulnerable, welcoming, warm, sincere, direct, honest—and still have high expectations. If you are not willing to address the specifics to high expectations, then you are not being humane.

Hitting your goals and metrics—whether you're an individual contributor, a manager, or a leader—is crucial, and it's significant for how you build your or your team's skills and confidence so that you can maintain results. A lot more goes into creating or choosing the right methodology and sales process than many people think. If you simply choose one because that's the one that everyone else is using, then you might be doing it wrong. While your company may claim to be the "world leader in_____," I can assure you that you are not, period. And if you are simply doing a copycat of what someone else is doing, you definitely are not a leader. You are merely a follower.

All of this *imperfection* is what really explains why sales is the greatest profession in the world. Once you realize and accept that it's never going to be perfect but can always be perfected, and once you accept there is always something to learn, and you are willing to commit, that is when you know you will be successful. The road to success is paved over the potholes of risk-taking, mistakes, mini-wins, and an open mind.

For the Sales Leaders

It can be hard to implement changes to the team and get their buy-in when they're not feeling confident in their sales skills.

And this is the purpose of this book. To help you and others around you build courage and confidence for yourself or your teams while gaining actionable skills, so when you and your team are in the trenches, it becomes easier to see a successful way out.

My approach to business and sales has always been aligned with servant leadership and processes. At my company, The Harris Consulting Group, making it about the prospect and customer has been in our foundation since day one. Making sure we can have human-to-human conversations has always been critical to our core beliefs as well as our sales training. We teach reps how to earn the right to ask questions, which questions to ask, and when. The COVID pandemic just confirmed what we already knew and have been teaching for years: when the pandemic hit, it felt like many people finally understood what it meant to be more empathetic to another human being. (Separate of the politics, of course).

Everyone knew someone who had COVID. This led many organizations to both subconsciously and consciously realize that how you talk to someone who is dealing with big changes matters. It's personal, it's emotional, and sometimes it's not easy.

During the pandemic, more organizations started seeking sales training because they finally realized that when you take a moment to genuinely speak with someone, the entire conversation becomes more personal, meaningful, healthy, and engaging.

However, over the same few years, everyone's been using the buzzword "growth mindset." And for the record, I hate buzzwords. The reason I hate them is that while they capture one's attention, the definition of that buzzword can be different for the person saying it than it is for the person hearing it.

And with this in mind, here's how I see the phrase "growth mindset." In the context of this book, we define growth mindset as a sharing mindset: when we share, we also open our minds up to learning, and that is where the growth can come from. We share our knowledge and wisdom.

It didn't happen when I was going through sales— it just didn't exist. The successful salespeople didn't know how to explain what made them successful, and even if they did know, they would never share the *secrets*. And many times when they knew, they would simply say, "Uhhh, well, I don't know." Even though they did. But now the mindset has completely shifted. Now we give away our knowledge and wisdom. Why? Because it's the human and humane thing to do. I want to help people to be better, so why not? The more I help others, the more they will want to help me. And even when they don't help me, they actually do. They help me by staying out of my way so that those who do want to reciprocate have an easy path. It's the long tail. This is humanity, not selfishness, and not manipulation. This is the sharing mindset.

My hope is that anyone who's really curious and interested in maintaining a sales growth mindset will be in a sharing mindset to help others and encourage others to share and learn. Pay. It. Forward.

We're All in This Together

I don't expect everything in this book to be perfect and work every single time, and I hope that by sharing these things we all get better. We try, we adapt, we evolve—and we approach a growth mindset. As we share together, we grow together, and the more I invested in my life or career in sales, the more I realized how badly we all need that to thrive not by ourselves, but together. #Humanity

Twenty-ish years ago, I started on the trek of really, truly learning and understanding myself. My history, my upbringing, the way that I tick... everything. And my personal journey really turned into my professional journey.

I'm sharing all of this because I didn't always have an open mind. I was old-school. I didn't share, and I definitely did not see the value in sharing. In short, I was an asshole. Over time and through a lot of reconnecting with myself, I learned how great the opportunity is and how much value there is in continuing to learn. On the personal side, it's wanting people to know they're not alone, and that also works for the professional side too.

I call this being a *per-fessional*—a combination of *personal* and *professional*—because, at the end of the day, we're one whole being. Our personal selves blend with our professional selves, so it's not about each of those personalities being at odds with one another. It's about turning to thinking, How can we make the two more harmonious?

Right now we need more humanity in sales than ever before. We are constantly bombarded with so much negativity in life. So many people like being experts and so many people are embracing anger as if tone of voice increases the rationality of their position. This is disappointing. We can disagree without being disagreeable.

We must take the steps to bring humanity back into the sales world, embrace it, and never let it go.

Better? Faster? Cheaper? More Human

Companies are always wanting to do things better, faster, and cheaper. Unfortunately, they can only do two at a time very well. If they claim they can do cheaper and faster, it won't be better; cheaper and better won't be faster; and better and faster won't be cheaper. But where is humanity in all of this?

Once a company understands that cheaper isn't always cheaper—that sometimes spending money now means you aren't paying more later in either dollars or human capital—then they begin to understand humanity.

Once a company understands that faster isn't always faster—that sometimes you may delay a part of the strategy so you can develop it more, and that's actually cheaper and faster in the long run—then they begin to understand humanity.

But it's a tough needle to thread. Finding the right balance between doing it right and doing it right now is not easy. Especially when we don't have a compass to guide us on our path.

For the last decade or so, sales has been focused on improving effectiveness and efficiency with the better tools at our disposal—what's often called the sales stack. Many of these tools are table stakes and should be required when taking a job. But they have made us better in some ways and worse in others. They have definitely improved efficiency, but they have not helped with effectiveness. In fact, one could argue they have done us a disservice and practically eliminated the humanity.

People will do business with us not just because of what we do; they will do business with us because of *how* we do it: the human-to-human relationship. As important as the human-to-human interaction is during the sales conversation, equally important is how they feel about us as people after the meeting.

Whether you've been in sales for twenty years or two, you know the profession is always evolving. As I write this book, in the spring of 2023, generative AI is just starting to get real attention in the sales community, not just prospecting. And I see people making the same mistake with AI that they made with other sales enablement platforms: they are thinking it can help them go better, faster, and cheaper, and they are forgetting all about the humanity.

Over the last twenty years, I've been able to witness sales from both the selling and buying side for companies. I've been able to dive deep into different structures of sales organizations and pull apart what works and what doesn't, maintain integrity, and allow each salesperson to be their authentic self—their own self-realized human. And I've developed the compass and map that will help guide you on the most impactful and positive Seller's Journey possible: N.E.A.T. Selling.

This Is N.E.A.T. Selling™

When we speak about the humanity in sales, it's important to understand all buying decisions are deeply personal and emotional. That is where they start, and that is where they end, period. As my friend James Harbeck once told me, humans are big bags of feelings with a brain that creates narratives and justifications for following the feelings, and experiences are things you feel something about—that's why you're motivated by them and remember them. When we recognize this, we recognize the humanity.

We (sales and marketing professionals) build the journey so that our prospects and customers have an amazing experience. That's what matters most. The Seller's Journey must *enhance* the Buyer's Experience. This is what we mean by humanity in sales.

So we like to put the two together using three perspectives:

1 **Situation:** We assess the situation using N.E.A.T. Selling. This is our compass.

2 **Relationship:** We understand the relationship with our prospects and customers by understanding the ego and using Respect Contracts. These contracts are followed by our company, our crew, and the people we are going on the journey with.

3 **Methodology:** We enhance communication through a method of specific tactics and soft skills. This is our map and our guidebook—and our equipment and techniques.

This book goes through all of these. If you do the hard work on them, you'll connect better, make more good sales, and everyone will be happier. You and your sales process will be more human.

Before I introduce you to N.E.A.T. Selling and tell you the details of it, however—before I even tell you what N.E.A.T. stands for—I want to address a fundamental question about what kind of thing it is I'm showing you: is it a philosophy, a methodology, or a process? The answer to this question is: yes.

Sales Philosophy

A sales philosophy is your commitment to your growth mindset as a sales professional. It is built on top of your values and culture. And it is used to guide how you treat people, which means your sales teams, your prospects, and your customers. It is your pathway to revenue.

A sales philosophy includes principles like these:

- The Customer Is Always Right
- Coffee Is for Closers

- Smile and Dial
- Earn the Right to Ask Questions

If you see N.E.A.T. Selling itself as your philosophy, we define that as "Teaching your reps how to earn the right to ask questions, which questions to ask, and when to do it." Or just call it #EarningTheRight.

As a philosophy, this can always be bolted onto your current sales methodology or process.

Sales Methodology

A sales methodology is a specific set of guidelines and strategies used to carry out the sales philosophy and talk with the prospect. It helps give balance to the process and reduce noise in a meaningful way that aids the opportunity in proceeding to close. The methodology is about how you will take someone through the Seller's Journey.

Examples of sales methodologies include:

- Spin Selling
- Challenger
- MEDDIC
- N.E.A.T. Selling

Sales Process

Essentially, the sales process is what you will do to give people the experience you want them to have as they go through their decision-making process.

A sales process must include the different emotional experiences—the most important of which is typically *trust*—that you want them to feel as they evaluate you and your services. Therefore, as you build your sales process, it's important to make sure you have the exit criteria in each stage.

By exit criteria, I mean a specific piece of information gathered or an activity that indicates a step forward in the process. Examples include demo scheduled or demo completed, pricing discussed, pricing confirmed, customer confirms you are short-listed as a potential vendor.

When defining your sales process, it's important to remember that the stages of your process are not actual activities. "Demo" is not a stage in the sales process. Neither are "Proposal," "Economic Buyer Identified," "Champion Identified," or "Redlining." These are all activities that occur within the sales process; in some cases, they are the actual exit criteria.

Your Choice

So, for your own needs and your company's, you may choose to see N.E.A.T. Selling as more of a philosophy, a process, or a methodology.

As an example, if I'm working with a larger enterprise company like Visa, they might view N.E.A.T. Selling as more of a philosophy attached to their existing process, and less of a full overhaul of their current one. As a larger organization, they might already have strict sales processes full of required fields they need to update in their customer relationship management (CRM) software, specific ways they need to do those updates to make them count, and they may even have very clear scripting that they don't want people to iterate on. N.E.A.T. Selling bolts on to help remind the team to drive Economic Impact within their existing sales process.

Meanwhile, other clients might love N.E.A.T. Selling because it breaks the complex into small, meaningful, easy-to-understand steps. Even for larger enterprise and complex sales cycles with ten or more decision-makers from various departments, it helps them align strategic outcomes with a powerful customer experience. And they can still use what's in their CRM if they so desire. At the core, N.E.A.T. Selling helps each of them in their own way to bring a little humanity to sales.

No matter how you decide to view or execute N.E.A.T. Selling principles, all the concepts taught here will work for any person in sales, any sales process, and any sales methodology. And as a bonus, these are life skills too. Which is a huge part of how and why I started N.E.A.T. Selling in the first place.

Do *Not* Rip and Replace!

What's at the core is a guiding principle. I created N.E.A.T. Selling to bridge the strategic and tactical silos to improve the Buyer's Experience and seller's mindset. The desired end result is to utilize N.E.A.T. Selling to improve trust, forecasting accuracy, close ratios, and revenue growth.

The advantage to adopting N.E.A.T. Selling is that it's *not* a rip-and-replace solution for your current process.

What we've found working with dozens of teams over the years is that when there is a problem with an existing sales process, it typically means that they haven't been coaching what's already created. All too often a new sales leader comes in and decides to rip and replace the current process. Wrong! Bad idea! Hard stop!

Organizations spend months rolling out newly vetted processes meant to help guide teams to close more revenue, and there will always be a multitude of different ways to achieve the same outcome. They call a meeting; maybe it's an hour, or god forbid maybe it's part of the sales kickoff (SKO). And they simply get it wrong, thinking this is all it takes to make the change (#SteakKnives!).

So why do so many sales leaders rip and replace? One simple answer: their ego. They have promised to part the Red Sea and deliver everyone to the Kingdom of the IPO. And last we heard, the average tenure for a VP of Sales is somewhere around sixteen months.

Now don't get me wrong, a sales process is a must. And yes, it can always be tweaked and improved. But changing it every year? Where is the humanity in that? In fact, it's inhumane because the change is merely about some leader's desire to feel better about themselves because they know they only have sixteen months to prove themselves before the next one comes along (#SteakKnives!).

So, which of these is more humane? Imagine you're at your SKO. Would you prefer learning a whole new process and all the new fields because your dashboard won't really change that much but the executives will, or would you prefer spending an hour learning how to negotiate with someone in a procurement department?

Can you imagine walking into a company like Visa and telling them to change everything in the CRM?

Can you imagine the Economic Impact that would create with all the changes to reporting and dashboards? Or how it affects all the different departments, then how long it will take to implement? Then how long it will take to onboard everyone into the "new way"? It's exhausting just thinking about it. Maybe it's necessary at times. But we think it's mostly a way for consultants to sell a huge services contract.

How Not to Fail

Let me repeat this: when I see *any* sales process fail, it's most likely because there isn't significant training, coaching, and reinforcement of the sales skills needed to achieve the desired outcomes.

If it's not being reinforced and coached by leadership on a regular basis, it's going to fail. From the least experienced reps who love coaching to the veteran salty dogs and Grumpy Guses, if you do not coach and reinforce, it will fail.

We've entered this new phase as companies and sales organizations in the last decade where our options and choices are multiplying constantly. Whether it be for trainers, coaches, methodologies, tools, products... whatever it is, we have endless options.

Sellers and leaders are iterating on sales processes regularly, or they should be at least. But if the consistency and reinforcement isn't there, it's not going to stick. If you're a sales leader, the power of continual emphasis on your sales process is going to boost your team's results so long as your approach is aligned with the sales process that's needed or in place at that moment.

It's OK to leave what you have and let N.E.A.T. Selling take over from there. You can have your teams follow another process while N.E.A.T. Selling supplements everything you are doing in your CRM. And by not making changes to the CRM, you are not wasting time (and Economic Impact) on reconfiguring all the reports and dashboards.

Remember: N.E.A.T. Selling can be a philosophy, a methodology, or a process, as you see fit. It's an add-on to bring an additional layer of flavor and value to what you're trying to accomplish.

{ 2 }

The N.E.A.T.
Selling Compass

N.E.A.T. SELLING IS ALL about trust. Nothing more, nothing less.

Our goal in sales is to help our customer "fall in trust" with us. Not fall in love—falling in love happens *after* the sale when they start using the product or service. At a personal level, our happiest purchases are those we've made where we *trust* the salesperson. So the single most important thing we can do in the sales process is build trust. And you build trust by understanding your customers—their needs and their pain points. Which means doing good discovery.

Is your team bad at creating urgency? Do you wish your sales team was better at negotiating and not giving away discounts? Do you wish they didn't have so many proposals out with no responses? Do you hate having to sift through the bullshit in your CRM on a Sunday night because there are too many deals that shouldn't be there? This all means your team is not doing proper discovery. They are merely talking about surface pains and headaches. Not core pains and migraines.

How your team thinks about N.E.A.T. Selling is as integral to its success as the reinforcement of it. It's less about adding steps to the process and more about helping them understand it.

Buying isn't buying—buying is simply decision-making. In fact, it's a process by which we reduce the risk we feel during our decision-making process so that in the end something is actually purchased. And as salespeople, our job is to help people reduce that feeling of risk they experience when making a purchasing decision. And if you're a sales leader, your job is to help your sales team reduce the risk they feel in trying something you've coached them on.

Think back to a time when you had to make a big purchase. Maybe you were buying a house, or a car, or software for your team. Whatever it was, think about the process you went through to sign off on that final decision (or not). We've all been buyers before, so when we go to make a purchase, we understand what it feels like to be trapped in a lousy sales process or cycle. You know, the kind that makes you walk away swearing to never go through the hassle again.

As sellers, even if we've experienced that buyer's pain before, we might get labeled as pushy, untrustworthy, or impatient. Buyers can feel when you're aching to make the sale and hit your quota; they can sense your intention. They smell blood in the water and they are thinking about how much fun it's going to be to drive you to a huge discount.

But that's not what creates an impactful Buyer's Experience. The goal throughout your process needs to move from being self-serving to adopting an experience-based, buyer's-mindset approach. It's all about building a foundation of trust by listening to and truly discovering your customers' needs. And many times our customers don't realize what they really need. They think they know, and they simply do not.

Think about how well you and your team really know your customer's needs and pains. Can you identify them by actual use cases, or just by buzzwords? If it's buzzwords, you are not actually understanding their core needs and pains. The goal is to understand the prospects' pains based on their current needs and actual experiences so you can quickly eliminate the prospects that aren't a good fit for your solution. Remember that disqualifying equals qualifying: getting rid of the disqualified prospects and opportunities provides more time to spend on new prospects and the best opportunities.

As with any journey, you need to know where you are when you start, and you need to confirm or correct where you are as you go. You need a compass. And in sales, the compass that tells you where things stand is not labelled North, East, South, West. This compass is labelled N.E.A.T.: Need, Economic Impact, Access to Authority, Timeline.

Need

The first N.E.A.T. Selling compass point focuses on the customer's needs.

- People do not care what you do. They only care about the pains you solve—and if you can solve their pains specifically.

- When determining your customer's needs, your goal is to get them to paint a picture of pain. People buy pictures, not words. It's our job to help them determine if their pains are simply headaches or actual migraines.

We still see people conducting weak discoveries.

When discussing a prospect's or client's needs, too many salespeople talk about what their product or service does, which naturally turns into a feature/benefit sales pitch. It means they are focusing on surface pains, not core pains. What's the difference? Surface pains are simply headaches. Core pains are migraines. And when someone has a migraine, there is an immediate moment of realization that makes curing this pain a greater priority than it was before the conversation started.

Painting a Picture of Pain

Believe it or not, people buy the pictures in their head more than the words they read or hear. We interpret the words and create an image in our minds so it's easier to understand. Pictures of pain equal use cases.

When a salesperson tries to paint the picture for the prospect, it's harder for them to relate. When a salesperson asks questions that help the prospect paint their own picture, they understand it intuitively.

So when this process reveals a core pain, that means you've asked your prospect the right questions for them to paint an accurate picture of pain in their own experience. Even if we know the picture ourselves, they need to hear themselves say it out loud to paint their own picture.

When they can describe a specific use case, that's when you are getting deeper to core pains. For example, if my prospect is the head of sales, I know they will probably be on their computer on Sunday nights sifting through the CRM and trying to answer the "Are you almost done?" question from their boo without saying, "No, it's going to be two more hours." Now when you ask them if something like this happens to them, that's where you know you found a real migraine, not just a headache. And from here the conversation naturally flows to the dollarization of the pain. (More on this when we get to Economic Impact.) (And for all the boos reading this: we are saying the work is the migraine, not the boo.)

So, is this a headache, or a migraine?

Discovery Questions

We believe it is important that you ask these questions of each person you speak with at every step of the way through the sales cycle.

For example, you may have an initial call with someone who will then report back to the buying committee or their boss. You may then need to have a conversation with the boss or committee.

Each time a new person joins the conversation, we recommend you summarize the current needs that were expressed and determine their specific needs as they relate to the project overall.

Here are some of the Need questions we recommend:

- What made you want to take this call today?
- What has happened recently to make you want to investigate this further?
- What is making this an issue now (insert current month/year) vs. twelve months ago?
- How often is this happening?
- What would "better" look like?

Economic Impact

The compass's second point is about the Economic Impact of the needs discussed.

- Have your customer paint pictures of pains to explain their challenges and then provide a current and future dollar or numerical value based on their own stories and their own data.

- Ask questions about the current way they are handling things, and determine the costs of their current state.

This allows you to show the true value of your solution in relation to solving their pains. And it gets them to confirm that what you offer is better, and by how much. And that means dollarization.

For example, oftentimes people want to be more effective and efficient. First, those are buzzwords, and I hate buzzwords. I hate them because when salespeople hear them, they make assumptions that the prospects' or customers' definitions of those buzzwords align with the value prop being presented to them. Even if they do align, it's still not a big enough pain to confirm they will purchase your solution. When we hear buzzwords like this, our goal must be to get the prospect to paint their ineffectiveness and inefficiency as real-world issues in their own words and provide the numbers that capture the dollarization of the pains they have. This allows the prospect to paint a new picture of what will happen when a calmer and better future state takes hold. How much better will it really be for them and the organization? In short, we want them to tell us about their migraines, not their headaches.

Now, how do we guide customers through this process? By asking better questions.

Here's an example:

Your client shares that they are wasting ten hours per month on a manual sales process. You dig deeper and discover it involves five of their sales reps, so it's really fifty hours per month wasted. Six hundred hours per year. *Six... hundred... hours!!*

We can easily dollarize based on salary.

So that's Economic Impact 1.0. Now here are the next three levels.

First, you ask your prospect, "Hey, if we can get you 75 percent—450 hours—of your sales team's time back, what would they do with that time?"

The answer is usually something like, "More sales."

Don't stop, dig deeper.

- How many reps will this affect, again?
- How many more deals per rep?
- And what's the lifetime value of each customer?

You now have Economic Impact 2.0.
Don't stop, dig deeper.

- OK, so if your team closes that much more, what does that do to your income?

- OK, does that mean you could go for a promotion or find a new job with a bigger title and salary?

- OK, so your company now has a higher valuation. Does that make it easier to get the next round of funding?

You now have Economic Impact 3.0.
Don't stop, dig deeper.

- OK, so your company now has $300,000 more to spend. What projects would your company spend it on?

- OK, will you be able to complete these projects three to six months faster?

- OK, if you can speed up these projects and get them completed three to six months sooner, what happens to your company?

    ◦ Are you now selling a new product or service?
    ◦ Are you upselling and cross-selling current customers?

You now have Economic Impact 4.0, which is the urgency they need to face.

Discovery Questions

This is where most deals are won and lost, in our opinion. This is the dollarization conversation. These are the "showing value" questions that translate into real numbers.

And the best part of this: when you ask the right questions, the dollars being discussed are *their* dollars. The prospects and customers *finally* admit to and hear their real pains. Their pains in their own words and their own dollars.

When you get to the dollarization answers, this will make any discounting conversations so much easier for you. It is hard for them to argue the need for a discount when you can simply state, "I'm confused.

When we spoke you said this pain is costing you $_____. In fact these are the numbers you gave me. So, what's the need for a discount exactly?"

Below are some of the Economic Impact questions we recommend asking based on certain goals of your prospects. Of course you should create your own, based on the pains you solve for your prospects/customers.

And just like the questions you asked during Need discovery, each time a new person enters the conversation we recommend you ask them specific Economic Impact questions as well. You will often uncover more dollarizations.

When the goal is to increase sales:

- What is your current sales cycle?

- What is your average contract value (ACV)?

- What is a current customer's lifetime value (LTV)?

- What does your desired growth mean exactly?

  ◦ **Improved cash flow:** if it improves cash flow, what could you do with that additional cash?

  ◦ **Hiring more:** if you hire more, what is the Economic Impact of those people getting on-ramped?

○ **Valuation:** if you grow by X percent, what does that do for your valuation? Could you get your next round of funding sooner?

When the goal is saving time:

- How many people are on your team?

- How much time does it currently take each person to accomplish this activity per week?

- So your total people-hours each week for this activity is _____, correct?

- What's the average salary per person for those affected?

- What other projects could these people be working on if they had more time?

- If we can get back _____ hours per month, what would your team do with that time?

- If those projects get completed sooner, what would that mean to the growth of your company?

Access to Authority

The N.E.A.T. compass's third point focuses on accessing the most influential people.

- Determine who the most skeptical people are on the decision-making committees.
  - Find out what they are most skeptical about.
  - Provide the necessary information for your champion to deliver to the skeptic.
- Determine if your contact has the juice to get you in front of the other influencers and the actual economic buyer.

When you are communicating with a buyer, you are not communicating with just one buyer. There is no longer a single decision-maker when it comes to buyers.

All purchases are made through a multitude of communities within your prospects' and customers' organizations. Some may actually be committees, while others will simply be a community of those affected by the decision. In either case, their blessing is required to close your sale.

Therefore, it's up to you to determine whether the person you are speaking with is merely a cheerleader or if they can actually champion your cause for you and get you access—specifically, Access to Authority. We define authority as the people who can approve a purchase. They will come in various flavors and personalities. You must understand them all, and specifically what makes them tick at a business level when it comes to making decisions.

Old-school sales philosophy was to get to the decision-maker as fast as possible. And we would, and still do, try to create an "internal champion," and then hope we have the right fairy dust to sprinkle to get a meeting with their boss or boss's boss. But the new school says we have to have a champion to help us determine the skeptics and the supporters. If they cannot help, then we merely have a cheerleader.

So what's the difference?

- A champion shares all information willingly and transparently, guides you through the entire selection process, and introduces you to the right people at the right time.

- A cheerleader only tells you what you want to hear about them being the champion, delivers nothing, and definitely cannot sign anything.

When looking for a champion, you have to know: does this person have the juice, the skill, the tenure, and the will to navigate this treacherous terrain? If we have a map that shows us where the quicksand, the pit of vipers, and the river of alligators are, it is helpful. In sales, we know danger zones exist; we simply don't have the map of them quite yet. So we are essentially Lewis and Clark on their first expedition, and your contact at the company is Sacagawea teaching us how to find the right path.

We need to figure out these danger zones faster. This means we need to know who the skeptics are more than anything else.

Let me say it louder for the people in the back of the room. We want to know the skeptics *first*! They will be the ones who prevent the sale, which is why they are as important to understand as the people who want our products or services.

Stop trying to figure out who signs the contract— figure out who can block the signature!

People are scared to make decisions by themselves, especially when that decision is a direct component of their job. They want to cover their ass so if something doesn't go right, they don't shoulder all the blame. So buying has now become a consensus exercise.

Sometimes the advisors are formal committees. Other times they are simply internal communities, those that have no structure but can be affected by the decision to purchase your products and services. And that decision affects a host of other people, including their direct reports and often other departments as well. Sometimes the purchase requires help or support from other teams like marketing, security, or IT. But the decision-maker is in the spotlight if the wrong thing is chosen. And it can be worse if they do not take other departments into consideration when those departments' regular duties, tasks, and business priorities are affected. It's comparable to how, as consumers, we regularly seek the counsel of others when making decisions.

Here are some of the decision-making committees or communities we see come up during the Access to Authority conversations with prospects and customers.

- **Vendor Selection Committee (possibly known as the Buying Committee):** the group that looks at which vendors to short-list and then approve.

  - **End User Influencers:** not a part of the committee but the people trialing your product/ service, who often have the heaviest influence on selection.

- **IT/Security Committees:** sometimes the same department, sometimes one is a subsidiary of the other.

- ◦ **IT Review Committee:** the group that makes sure your stuff doesn't break their stuff.
- ◦ **Security Review Committee:** the group that ensures all legal compliance issues are accurate.

- **Legal Committee:** the team that approves the contract.

- **Finance Committee:** the team that actually writes the check. This could be:
  - ◦ **CFO:** the person who loves to scare the salesperson and gives final pricing approval.
  - ◦ **Procurement Team:** the group that loves to scare the salesperson and gives final pricing approval.

Now this might be counterintuitive, but here is what *not* to ask: "Who controls the budget?" or "Who else needs to approve it?" or "Who will actually sign the contract?"

Instead, ask this: "Who is the most skeptical person on the team? And what are they most skeptical about?"

And remember, we already know that after every meeting there is *another internal meeting* that we are never a part of. So here is how we coach people.

1 "Hey John, I know you are going to have to take this back to your team for their opinion at some point. I am curious: who on the team is typically the most skeptical person?"

2 "OK, when you think about them, what would you say they will be skeptical about when you bring this forward?"

3 "OK, so if they are skeptical, and you love it, what happens when there is not alignment in that scenario?"

Discovery Questions

Often people love to use the word "review," as in "legal review" and "security review." Whether it's intentional or unintentional, a salesperson hears these phrases and gets nervous because it feels like some big Judgment Day team. And that's fair to feel. All feelings are fair.

We encourage salespeople to remember that these "reviewers" are really just people like you and me—a single person or an entire group. They are not really the Big Bad Wolf, and you are not Little Red Riding Hood. People are people.

Here are some of the questions we recommend salespeople ask during the Access to Authority phase of the sales process:

- When you take this back to your team for approval, who is the most skeptical person on the buying committee?
    - What are they typically skeptical about the most?
    - What type of information do they like to see that helps them feel more comfortable making the decision?
- What other teams are affected by this decision?
- What other departments should we consider as you look to move forward?
- Is there anyone going on vacation or taking a leave throughout this process?
- What internal resources are required to actually implement this?
- Does someone from IT need to approve this?
    - Who is that and who will be able to tell them to make this a priority?
    - What other projects might they have that could delay this decision?

- Does someone from Security need to approve this?
  - Who is that and who will be able to tell them to make this a priority?
  - What other projects might they have that could delay this decision?
- Does someone from Accounting need to approve this?
  - Who is that and who will be able to tell them to make this a priority?
  - What other projects might they have that could delay this decision?
- When does Legal get involved?
  - Who is that and who will be able to tell them to make this a priority?
  - What other projects might they have that could delay this decision?
- Who will be the main point of contact internally to shepherd all these approvals?

Timeline

The fourth and final point on the compass is about dealing with timelines—and the need to be diligent when doing so.

- The timeline is not defined by the date the contract will be signed.

- The timeline is defined by the date when the prospect expects to start onboarding your product or services.

- If you do not have Economic Impact and Access to Authority clearly defined, then any timeline discussed is merely a line in the sand that will get washed away with the changing tides.

No deal can be closed without knowing when it's going to close, but this is merely a seller's point of view. The buyer's point of view focuses on when they can actually get their hands on the product to do the things they want it to do.

So many times we—including me—believe our prospects when they give us a timeline. We hear a date and assume it's true, but our job is to confirm repeatedly. Essentially, we hear what we want to hear, and once we have it, we don't want to do or say anything that might make it worse. This is what someone once called "Happy Ears." We don't hear what is actually being said.

We ask a prospect things like, "Great, when would you like to get started? When are you seeking to implement?"

The prospect gives us a date.

And we do a hard stop and start doing our ritual closing dance because we got a date. But that is premature.

We must dig deeper.

Here is what we typically teach to our clients. It's often a multilayered approach to digging and getting closer to the core:

1   What happens if you don't implement by [date]? If there is no real pain, then you have not done a good enough job on Need and Economic Impact, or have not gotten Access to Authority.

2   OK, so to get launched by then, how long will it take to get approval?

3   OK, so to get launched by then, how long will the legal process take?

4   What other internal projects could come up to delay this moving forward?

Discovery Questions

Most salespeople and sales leaders simply suck at timeline discovery. This is because they focus too much on just one of the timelines: "What day will we get the signed contract back?"

And then what happens?

The deal pushes to the next month or quarter. Or evaporates entirely.

And then what happens?

We are shocked.

And then what happens?

Our bosses and bosses' bosses are shocked too and become "bossy blamers" looking for scapegoats.

(A special note for all the bossy bosses and bossy blamers: if this has happened more than once in your career, then it's categorically, undeniably your fucking fault! You keep complaining that it happens, and it's still happening? Why haven't you fixed it?)

You know there's this cool thing called the internet, right?

And you know you can ask it questions, right?

And you know it will give you good answers, right?

And you're in leadership so therefore you must know how to take an idea to the masses, right?

Oh, wait, my bad. You don't know any of this stuff. Thanks for buying the book. Let me know if you need me to come to train your team.

In case I haven't been clear: it's not the salesperson's fault for a deal pushing if their sales leaders have not taught them about qualifying Timeline. If your deals push, short of some significant and unexpected life event happening to your prospect, like a family illness, then you've got Fake Timelines.

A Fake Timeline is what you get if you just take the "Reverse Engineer the Timeline" approach, which goes something like this: "So when do you want to implement this? Great, to implement by [date], it typically takes us __ weeks for the integration and onboarding. With this in mind, we would need to get the contract signed by [date]. Can we do that?"

Now don't get me wrong, these are good questions to ask. However, too many salespeople and sales leaders simply stop there and never get to the real timeline. Yes, it is always important to know the timeline from the prospect's perspective. However, a deal signature timeline is based upon several Mini-Timelines.

Mini-Timelines are the specific moments when resources are committed by both parties to move a deal to closing. They can include anything from demos and deep-dive demos to competitor conversations, legal resources, financial resources, etc. If you only do a reverse timeline, then you are missing out on the real things that can move the deal forward.

And in addition, unless there is significant financial pain felt by the person and organization from missing the proposed launch date, there again you'll have a Fake Timeline.

Here are some questions we encourage people to ask when it comes to *confirming* real deal signature dates:

- What is your desired implementation date?

    ◦ What are the negative impacts if you do not implement this by [date]?

- How long does your approval process normally take?

    ◦ How long do you think it will take your committees to give internal approval? (Selection, IT, Security, Legal Committees—ask about all of them.)

    ◦ Who could prevent this approval from happening?

- What else could prevent the signature from happening by [date]?

    ◦ What other internal projects can come up that would cause this one to be delayed?

The Compass

Sales is never linear. It ebbs and flows, like the tides. Some days there are clear and sunny skies. Other days are gloomy or stormy. And of course, there are days when our prospects and customers go completely dark.

This is the reason for the compass metaphor. The compass symbolizes that no matter where you are on the Seller's Journey, you can keep yourself oriented and on the right path. The N.E.A.T. Selling compass guides us no matter how we decide to utilize it—as a philosophy, process, or methodology.

Every customer is truly unique in their approach to whatever solutions we provide. And even if we don't have the same approach, we must meet them in their headspace. N.E.A.T. Selling allows us to take them on our Seller's Journey while also respecting them and providing them with an amazing Buyer's Experience.

Unlike other sales methodologies, N.E.A.T. Selling does not have a strict order. Not every sales conversation starts with N and then goes to E, A, and T, in that order. Sometimes a sales conversation starts with a deadline, a crisis, or a research effort. And while we can quickly move to Need, which is often the case, the conversation does not always start there. It is the situation that prompted the initial conversation that can then drive us to the need.

For example, sometimes our customers tell us they need sales training. Well, there is something that happened before they reached out to us that indicates the need exists. Often times it is something like missing quota or hiring new sales reps. This prompts a need for a conversation, with the specific type of conversation yet to be determined.

If someone says, "My boss told me to contact you," we may be starting with Access to Authority before we get into actual needs.

And if someone says they need sales training because they have a trade show coming up, we start with Timeline before diving into the type of needs they specifically want to address in the training.

We encourage you to find the right way to make the compass work for you, in a way that supports the Seller's Journey. And be sure to remember that the customer experience is what you want to enhance more than anything.

{ 3 }

The Process

NOW THAT WE HAVE the compass, where do we go with it? We understand that the process is about getting prospects to fall in trust with us, and we know that it's all about building a Seller's Journey that supports the Buyer's Experience, so how do we put everything together?

The first thing to understand about any sales process is conversational flow. What order should a sales conversation follow? And how do you do it so that the experience is wonderful for your prospects and customers?

One of the things you'll notice in the process's staging and naming is that no activity is the name of a stage. Any activity such as "demo" or sending a proposal is a part of the overall process and not the name of an actual stage. In fact, demos conducted or proposals sent are merely exit criteria from one stage to the next.

Let's quickly take a look at the breakdown of conversational flow and typical sales stages:

N.E.A.T. Selling Process

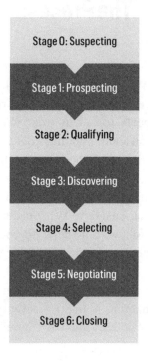

Stage 0: Suspecting

Stage 1: Prospecting

Stage 2: Qualifying

Stage 3: Discovering

Stage 4: Selecting

Stage 5: Negotiating

Stage 6: Closing

The first step in conversational flow is respect and trust. This is extremely important in the N.E.A.T. Selling process. We start our relationships with buyers by earning their trust so that we, in turn, earn the right to ask questions. In the coming chapters we'll dive more into how we can build respect by creating Respect Contracts, but right now let's look at the big picture of conversational flow. After we earn respect and trust, we start moving through the sales stages.

1 **Prospecting:** Prospects are the people with whom an actual communication exchange has occurred. It can be email, phone, social media, etc. The point is that these people have responded. Even if the answer was "not interested," they responded and therefore may be someone to contact in the future. When creating pipeline persona definitions, some clients use "suspects" or prospects for Stage 0. These are the people in your Ideal Company Profile and Ideal Persona Profile. Not all suspects are prospects.

2 **Qualifying:** Once a prospect has agreed to a first meeting, they are now in the qualifying mode. This means you are confirming they are the right company, the right person, the right department, or they provide Access to Authority as you need it.

No opportunity is considered "qualified" until it moves out of this stage and into discovery.

3 **Discovering:** This is when you start having real conversations about their actual pains. Where you get them to start telling you about headaches and migraines. Aside from going deep on Need, this is where you are driving to real Economic Impact, Access to Authority, and Timeline. It is not unusual for prospects to stay in discovery for longer periods of time.

4 **Selecting:** This is the part of the sales conversation where the prospect tells you that you are short-listed at minimum. It's where you know what the competition is, where they confirm the Economic Impact is real, and where worthy conversations about Commercial Terms begin. This is often when you confirm the approval process, start talking about the legal process, and confirm the timeline.

5 **Negotiating:** This is where Commercial Terms are finalized. What is the exchange of goods and services worth to them? Having done your discovery on Economic Impact really pays off in this stage.

6 **Closing:** This is where you send the contract for redlines, confirm how long the legal process takes,

and verify when you can expect to get the signed contract back.

Customer Success

The success of the SaaS (Software as a Service) model, which has annual contracts that renew each year, means greater attention is being paid to retaining current customers. So no book about sales can exist without acknowledging the importance of Customer Success, which is so often overlooked.

Customer Success became a recognized category in sales around 2011. Before this, it was often called Customer Support or Customer Service, and in that iteration was seen more like problem-solving. Traditionally, Customer Success started as the group that *onboards* new clients. They are the people who walk new users through the activation and use of the product or service. In addition they maintain regular contact to ensure the customer is utilizing the service with *best practices* in mind.

Since that time, the growth of a SaaS model has relied on the purchase of additional licenses or services during the contract period or at the time of renewal. This is called upselling or cross-selling the customer, which increases your company's revenue and growth as well as the sales relationship's "stickiness"—its ability to continue for the long term.

In SaaS, this is often referred to as the "land and expand" model. First you land the account with one group of people using the service, and over time you expand by having them purchase additional licenses to the service and/or additional services, both of which increase the revenue value to your organization.

When a client gets to the end of the annual subscription, the customer has a few choices:

1   Renew with the same number of licenses.

2   Renew and add new licenses or additional services or both.

3   Renew with fewer licenses and/or services.

4   Churn: not renew anything at all and stop using your service.

So, who is responsible for all of this—onboarding new clients, cross-selling and upselling current clients, and servicing and renewing clients?

There is constant dialogue on who should handle the cross-sell and upsell. Should it be a sales team or the Customer Success team? Oftentimes Customer Success teams are built with individuals who truly love digging in, helping customers achieve their goals, and do not mind handling the challenges a customer may bring up from time to time. And often these people are people-pleasers by nature. This is not a bad thing. It is a very good thing in fact.

People-pleasers need approval from others to sustain their own self-worth and value.

This does not mean these people are less valuable than anyone else. It is simply a part of their makeup. Can they be coached around this? Well, that is up to you, them, and anyone with a psychology degree to delve into.

So, who handles your cross-sell and upsell? It's simple: it's the people who are comfortable in the uncomfortable conversations. That does not mean unprofessional. It means they are comfortable talking about things like pricing, contracts, services, handling negotiations, etc. To make it even simpler, the answer will be very clear as you read the sales tactics and strategies in this book. Every tactic and strategy can be used in some form by the Customer Success team as much as they can be used by the sales team. The responsibility lies with the individuals who are the most comfortable following the guidelines provided here. If someone is not comfortable implementing the strategies in this book, they should not be responsible for the upselling and cross-selling initiatives of your organization.

Understanding Exit Criteria

For any sales process to be successful, we must understand and define the conversations and activities that need to happen throughout the process, and what their outcomes really are. These steps are the exit criteria.

On the surface, the goal of having exit criteria is to ensure better accuracy of business forecasting and, therefore, revenue. However, the real value of exit criteria is that they help sales leaders and salespeople understand where they can improve their own skills. The more specific and finite you can make an exit criterion, the easier it will be to identify where to help and coach your sales team and, of course, where your pipeline is the weakest.

Exit criteria must be something tangible that has happened or will happen. Here are a few examples:

- First meeting set
- First meeting completed
- Demo completed
- Commitment date and time from prospect to completion
- Verbal confirmation you have been short-listed
- Confirmation you understand decision-making process

- Confirmation you understand contract process
- Contract out for redlines

From my vantage point, having a defined next step after an activity is always the strongest exit criterion. Sales forecasts are always based on the information we have—and in some cases don't have. That information is your exit criterion.

We believe that reviewing the sales process and exit criteria at least two times a year ensures the best path for revenue growth. With startups or even mature companies that are rolling out a new product, it can be wise to review your sales process and exit criteria monthly for the first ninety days.

In each stage, there will be exit criteria to leave that stage and move forward, so what are they? What specific activities move the sale forward for your team? Is it having a call scheduled, completing a call, discussing something specific, talking about launch dates? Whatever it is, create exit criteria for every stage of the process.

For a visual display of how we view this, here's an example we share with clients on building their own sales process (adjust as you see fit):

Sales Process v.1	Ownership	Activity
Stage 1: Qualifying	• SDR/AE	• 1st meeting set; 1st meeting occurs
Stage 2: Discovering	• AE/SE	• 2nd+ meeting(s) set; 2nd+ meeting(s) occur • Demo(s) • Competition • Pains confirmed & clarified • Decision-making committee
Stage 3: Selecting	• AE/SE/Mgmt/ IT, Security, Legal, Procurement	• Pains confirmed & clarified • Competition • Pricing discussed • Purchasing group process • Decision approval process • Legal process • Security/IT approval process • Procurement process confirmed • Redlines sent
Stage 4: Negotiating	• AE/SE/Mgmt/ IT, Security, Legal, Procurement	• Pricing finalized • Legal process confirmed • Security/IT approval process confirmed • Purchasing group
Stage 5: Closing	• AE/VP/ C-level	• Redlines received • Final terms approved

Exit Criteria	N.E.A.T. Requirements (at minimum)
• 1st meeting set; Prospect schedules 2nd meeting	Need Access to Authority
• Prospect confirms specific pains & we can tie an economic impact to their current condition • Prospect accepts their pains as real, & our solution would make things better • Demo occurs • Skeptics identified	Need Economic Impact Access to Authority
• Competition was discussed & prospect can repeat back our differentiators • Understand the decision-making process and all players • Pricing discussed • Customer confirms our short-listed status • Security/IT issues resolved • Decision-making confirmed • Decision-approval process confirmed • Timeline confirmed by understanding what happens if the timeline is not met based on buyers' pains & economic impact	Need Economic Impact Access to Authority Timeline
• Customer says they want to purchase • Timeline for receiving contract confirmed • Contract out for redlines with a specific date on when to get them back • Deal desk approved	Need Economic Impact Access to Authority Timeline
• Contract sent for signature with an expected return date • Received signed contract	Need Access to Authority Timeline

One final point: as you build a sales process and include exit criteria, it will change over time. Think about it: as you talk to more people, as your products or services change, as the competitive landscape changes, or as economic factors shift, so should your process.

It's helpful to think about your sales process as a *hypothesis* that can change based on the collection of additional data. My most successful clients audit their sales process at least once per year, if not twice. And remember, a change in the process is *not* a change in sales methodology. It simply means you are checking that you are collecting the right data and adjusting exit criteria to fit with a desired outcome, which will improve forecasting and close ratios, reduce sales cycles, and increase contract values.

{ 4 }

Sales Is Always Personal

_____

MANY THINGS HAVE CHANGED in sales since the time (very long ago) when I started. Back then, we didn't have the tools and the guidance that teams do now to prepare for what could greet you on the other side of the sales call. But one thing stays the same: the dynamics between seller and buyer. It's an interaction between people. And the person who's in the driver's seat is you, the seller.

The biggest bullshit idea I hear repeated is that the buyers have more knowledge going into the process. This is simply a lie that people love to throw in our faces to try to scare and intimidate us.

Your buyers have far *less* knowledge than you.

And it's time we understand that and respect ourselves and all our hard work.

Let me explain. Buyers are considered to have more knowledge because they are more conditioned to a commodity purchase process, given the frequency and ease of purchasing just about everything these days in a commoditized and commercialized society. But the sellers have this much more buying experience too—we are consumers too! And the good news is that the sellers have even *more* knowledge thanks to the tools in our sales stack, the availability of training, and the ease with which an individual can take it upon themselves to improve. I mean, you're reading this book, right?

So in reality, the advantage lies with the salesperson. When you dig deeper and seek to improve your skills and learn more about your craft, and you are willing to practice, you end up being in a better position than the person on the other side of the table. After all, how many of your customers actually take courses and buy books to learn how to be better at buying?

But don't let this give you an attitude as you walk into the sales conversation. Watch your ego (more about that in a moment). Simply use this knowledge to help reset your courage and confidence in the career you've chosen to pursue. Respect yourself—you've earned the right. This is what we like to call an internal Respect Contract.

Your Whole Self

The old mantra of "leave your personal life at the door" when you walk into the office is not only old-school, it is simply wrong. Believe me—I used to live and coach to this mantra. It wasn't until I started investing in my own personal therapy and learning about the dynamics of the human condition that I was able to relate what I was learning back to the business world. And then I realized that we are whole beings. We bring our whole self wherever we go.

At work, we bring our professional self. In social situations, we bring our personal self. We are often taught to separate the two to achieve happiness. I'd like to encourage people to shift the mindset. You bring your whole self with you everywhere you go. And rather than separate them, you can choose to focus on one part of your being for a period of time. Whether we are building a team or a family, whether we are building a relationship with a prospect or a partner, we are whole beings and everything engages with everything else. The lessons learned in one relationship can and should help shape and improve the other relationships we have. Sometimes it goes our way; sometimes it does not. And in all cases, our whole being is better.

It took me a long time, and a lot of personal and professional success and setbacks—probably more setbacks than success—to reach this understanding. Hopefully I can help some folks get there faster. And it started with a journey to improve my personal self over my professional self.

Back when I first started out in therapy, I was trying to heal from my childhood and upbringing. Just so folks don't go wondering, "OMG, how bad was it?" I can assure you it was not all that bad. I was never abused, and my parents were not alcoholics or drug addicts. We were pretty typical for that time. My parents divorced when I was about ten, but it was amicable, no custody issues, and everyone still engaged in family gatherings and get-togethers. But that doesn't mean I wasn't affected. Like most people, I had some shit I had to deal with. Big props to my mom and dad for doing the work so that things could be relatively normal and for being very open and supportive throughout my journey.

And from that I started seeing a therapist. She changed my life, my whole life, my whole being. She helped me with my career and being a workaholic as well as my personal life. Without her I would not have my career, the ability to write this book, and most importantly my loving wife, two sons, and two dogs.

There were two early lessons my therapist taught me that I bring to the sales training world—what I teach and how I teach it.

First, she helped me understand what it means to respect yourself. Respect yourself based on where you are, not where you think you should be. In time, you can get to those other places; it's just much harder if you do not have an internal Respect Contract.

Very early on, maybe the first or second session, she said, "We are going to have fun with this." On the one hand I was like, "OK, that's cool, I like fun." On the other hand I was scared out of my mind and thinking, "What the fuck is going to be fun about me coming in here weekly and bawling?"

She was right: it was a lot of fun and continues to be to this day. What she knew and was trying to teach me, without giving it away, is that through my willingness to learn about myself, I was going to respect myself in ways I had never known—or at least remembered. It was my internal Respect Contract.

The second thing she taught me about was Transactional Analysis. I refer to this almost daily in my life, whether it's with prospects, customers, my family, or, yes, even myself. Transactional Analysis is how I watch my ego—and my customers' egos too.

Transactional Analysis: Parent, Adult, Child

Transactional Analysis is a theory and practice originated by Eric Berne, MD. It looks at the communication exchanges between people and theorizes that our childhood experiences have an immense impact on our lives as adults. (That might not be groundbreaking thinking nowadays, but back when I was diving into therapy it blew my mind.)

Berne suggested that during a conversation, we might unconsciously respond in ways that are influenced by past childhood experiences, anxieties, or emotions. He believed we have three different ways of interacting, or three different ego states: Parent, Adult, and Child. Berne believed that how we were raised affects how we develop our ego states.

When I first learned about this and let it sink in, I was blown away. It felt like when you're cleaning a room in your house where everything's sprawled all over the floor, covering every empty space, and you finally organize it and put it all away. You feel clear again. It was my first time truly connecting with and

Transactional Analysis: 3 Egos

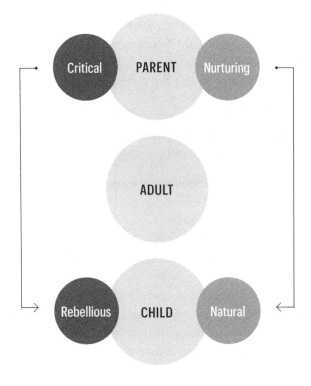

understanding myself. Not only did it help me heal some things I was struggling with internally, I found out how it gives us the key to understanding our personal and professional relationships, which is essential for creating Respect Contracts.

The ego states explain a lot of my work and how I approach my life and business, so let's get a deeper understanding of how exactly it connects.

Here's a quick and dirty explanation of Transactional Analysis.

The Child Ego: Beginning the Process

Feelings are a big part of the Child Ego state:

- It's where our feelings and emotions are stored
- Win a deal and feel good
- Lose a deal and feel bad
- Excited about the new TV
- Heart breaks when someone ends a relationship

The Child Ego state essentially says, "I want it," and this is where *all* decisions originate. It's built upon reinforcement we were given as kids: positive or negative, how we can behave or can't behave, what we get praise for or don't, etc.

Your customer wants to speak with you. Your customer wants a demo, or maybe they want a discount. That's their Child Ego speaking. Maybe you don't want to believe me about where decisions originate, and that's okay. It just means I proved the point—you don't *want* to believe me.

The Child Ego is where the Buyer's Experience begins.

The Adult Ego: The Rational Mindset

This is a more thoughtful state that weighs:

- Pros and cons
- Pluses and minuses
- Upside and downside

After considering the pros and cons of things, the Adult Ego gives us permission to move forward. Permission to pitch on a cold call, permission to set the first appointment, permission to send a contract. It's the here and now of any interaction; it's the place we operate from that allows us to listen fully, be more open, less quick to make harsh judgments. By the way, closed-ended questions force a rational mindset. Did you know that? See, that's one right there.

The Adult Ego state gives us permission to move forward.

The Parent Ego: The Safety and Self-Reflective

The Parent Ego passes judgment:

- Right vs. wrong
- Appropriate vs. inappropriate
- Good vs. bad

The Parent Ego is the one that protects you; it helps you feel safe. It's built upon reinforcements from our past, whether positive or negative, and affects our day-to-day interactions in the present. It's the piece of us that conforms in order to be seen in a certain way, but it can also be our rebellious side.

The Ego States in Selling, Part I

What on earth does all this have to do with sales? It's simple: sales is about people, and all people have these ego states. They are always there, and they'll never go away. This is another example of the humanity in sales.

Now, keep in mind that nobody stays in a single ego state very long. In fact, it's mere split seconds. We can start in a Child Ego state at the beginning of a sentence, shift into a Parent state midway through, and fall into an Adult state by the end. The states change instantly, without you even noticing in most cases.

Let's say you want to craft a message to a prospect or client.

Child: You decide you want to craft a good message.

Parent: You write it and judge it, and judge it, and judge it.

Child: You don't want to send the current version 'cause it sucks.

Adult: You start to rewrite it.

Parent: You judge again.

Adult: You craft a message you like.

Child: You want to send the message.

Parent: You judge again.

Adult: You give yourself permission to send the email.

See that whole conversation going on subconsciously with yourself? It happens within seconds. Now, imagine you write this email, and before sending it, you ask someone to take a look at it. They're going to go through all of these ego states themselves. Now, imagine you've done the demo and it's time for your prospect to go back and get it "reviewed as a team." That's a lot of ego states flying around. The process won't always flow in the order described; it's just an example to help you think and see how quickly they fluctuate.

So let's see it from your prospect's perspective:

Child: As the user of your product or service, they *love* it, they *want* it, but they may not have the juice to pull the trigger.

Child: Your prospect asks for a discount.

Adult: Final terms are agreed upon, and they tell you to send the contract over.

Child: They ask questions to compare you to your competition.

Parent: They take the competitive information and start judging it.

Adult: Based on competitive information, they decide to move forward with either you, your competitor, or neither of you.

Can you see how the ego states inform our conversations? The greatest practice is learning to be conscious about which state you're operating from, and allowing yourself to change it. I really began focusing on how important the ego states were back when I was starting out in sales. The power dynamics in business conversations were incredibly important to me. After I'd worked with sales teams and been able to see from the inside out how they operate, it became apparent how often sellers are operating from an ego state that kills their confidence and doesn't put them in a position of power. We're used to giving up our power immediately because we believe we're less than our prospects. If a sales rep is calling the CEO of a Fortune 500 company, they're not going to think for a second that they're operating on the same level as the CEO.

All of these ego states react with one another in different ways. Now think about being in a group sales call, where your prospect has three people, and you bring a team of three people. That is six people with their own ego states all flying around like crazy. They are always in play.

Now, I do not expect you to all of a sudden recognize the ego states in every call and conversation. My hope is to give you an inch of space between what your prospect is saying when they are in the Parent Ego state and what you are feeling in the moment.

Ego States in Selling, Part II

The Parent Ego can be broken down into two different sub-egos: the Critical Parent and the Nurturing Parent. The Child Ego also includes two sub-egos: the Natural Child and the Rebellious Child. (There is also an Adaptive Child sub-ego, as described below.)

The Critical Parent is exactly what you might think. It is that voice that is criticizing you, or perhaps you are interpreting it as critical. Your prospect may say, "Your competitor does this better than you" or "Why can't you do it this way?" You can recognize it as the same tone you hear when your mom comes to visit and tells you how to reorganize your kitchen, even though you've been on your own for thirty-plus years. Sorry, Mom, not sorry. But I digress.

Now, because we grew up with our parents or parental figures, when we hear "the tone" we naturally fall into a Child Ego state. And that state is either the Rebellious Child, who wants to tell someone to fuck off, or the Adaptive Child, who is being driven by fear, guilt, or shame.

In the case of our prospect, we want to start handling their objections, and we are caught somewhere between the Rebellious and Adaptive Child.

Now on the other hand, there is the Nurturing Parent. This is also what you think: it's the one who wants to help you solve a problem, fix the boo-boo, or find a way to work things out cordially.

And based on our upbringing, when we hear the Nurturing Parent, it most likely brings out the Natural Child. The Natural Child is, to put it simply, happy. It's perhaps a pleasant state of mind in the present moment. And when we get excited because we are getting something we want, the childlike joy is more apparent.

In a business conversation, it might be something like the prospect simply asking, "Hey, do you think we can do_____?" Tone of voice can have a lot to do with expressing the ego state in simple exchanges like this.

Now, here is the weird part to look out for.

Sometimes when I hear the prospect being a Critical Parent, which of course then makes me want to be a Rebellious Child, I have to remember that they are often responding to me. Though they sound like a Critical Parent, they are probably being a Rebellious Child because they are not getting what they want. In the pricing and discounting conversation, they are often bouncing between Parent and Child Ego states. Their Parent is trying to be critical of you and your service, and their Child wants a discount.

It is also possible that we could say something in a way that's simple—and, we hope, nurturing—but the prospect is hearing it as a criticism. One example of this would be when you have to deliver news the prospect does not want to hear. Perhaps a product issue, delayed release, or not being able to meet the pricing.

(And yes, email has made it much easier for everyone to be Critical Parents because they can hide behind their monitors and CPUs.)

One last example of the ego states. I am willing to bet most people reading this book sometimes feel like they have a closet full of nothing to wear. You may even have something in your closet that still has the tags on and you have never worn it. Maybe you bought it in a hurry and didn't have time to try it on. Maybe you liked how it looked online, and then when it got to you, it wasn't right.

Now, which ego state is preventing us from wearing these items? Parent? Partially. Adult? Maybe. But in most cases it's the Child.

Remember, the Child is where our emotions are stored. It's where buying decisions begin and end.

So why don't we like the item? Is it because of how it looks? No. Is it because of how it fits? No.

It's because of how it makes us feel. We don't feel good in it. We may not like how it fits, which means we don't like how it looks. But underneath all of this is how we feel about it.

Think about that with your prospects and customers. If they don't feel good about your product or service, or if they don't feel good about the Buyer's Experience, then their Critical Parent will probably not think your product or service is appropriate, and therefore the Adult Ego state cannot give them permission to move forward.

Now, this is a lot to absorb. I don't expect you to become a master of this information or recognize each ego state the moment it happens. But this knowledge can help you give yourself an extra inch of space between your brain and your heart. That space allows you to take a mental exhale and hopefully realize that people are people and none of us are perfect. This is an example of how we can actively bring humanity back into sales.

That's the thinking we have to develop to have stronger sales conversations, which is why I focus so heavily on Respect Contracts.

{ 5 }

Respect Contracts

———————

WE HAVE TO EARN the right to ask questions, know which questions to ask, and when to do it. But before we get into this more deeply, let's take a look at ourselves first.

In the last chapter we talked about decisions being emotionally based. Which also means they are emotionally *biased*—for both parties in the sales conversation. Bias is natural, and it's unavoidable. We are taught by parental figures and society that we should apply some level of rationality and logic to our actions, so what we do is layer reasoning on top of our emotions, which means the emotions give a particular slant to the reasoning. So everyone has biases. In fact, when we learn a new mindset, it's often simply a new bias taking over an old one.

This does not mean that our behaviors or biases are bad. It simply means they exist. And the moment we acknowledge this existence, we can effect real change in ourselves, and perhaps in our prospects and customers if they want to go on this journey and have this experience too.

When you look at it from a customer's perspective, they are already coming in with a bias against salespeople and/or the sales process, and yes, this can have a tinge of disrespect. Then we may end up feeling disrespectful towards them, although most likely we'll become sheepish, which means we do not respect ourselves.

So we want to create a new logical approach and a new emotional basis so we have a new sense of respect—respect for ourselves, and respect for our prospects and customers in such a way that they respect us. And when mutual respect happens, everything becomes so much easier.

Buy-In vs. Buying

Sometimes the resistance to the changes we face is internal. And that internal conflict means we have to buy in on a new way of doing things. Change may be hard because we feel like we are either consciously or unconsciously not respecting our current belief system.

This is where a Respect Contract comes in. There are several types of Respect Contracts—verbal, written, and digital. (These days written and digital are almost the same thing.)

A little history on the Respect Contract. Lots of sales training organizations teach this concept. And if you dig deep enough in history, you will see it's been around forever, or at least since biblical times.

Do you know how many times a Respect Contract was used in the Bible? It's almost too many to count.

Conversations between God and Adam, between God and Moses, between God and Noah—Respect Contracts are all over the place. One of the most interesting ones is the conversation between God and Abraham. In fact, instead of "contract," the word used was "covenant." Check them out. You will see the elements of what we call a Respect Contract: Time, Goals, Agenda, Potential Outcomes, Social Contracts, and a Transition statement to the rest of the conversation.

So no, we don't lay claim to the creation of this process—we simply modernized it for the sales world in the twenty-first century.

In sales, a Respect Contract is used to help create mutual respect between sellers and prospects or buyers. It's the first step in getting our prospects to fall in trust with us; we make sure everyone invests emotionally in a social contract so neither party feels pressured about the conversation or the potential decisions.

For a salesperson, a Respect Contract:

1 Gives the rep a way to respect their time, their role, and themselves.

2 Improves the courage and confidence we have to guide a prospect through our Seller's Journey and give them an amazing Buyer's Experience.

3 Allows reps to earn the right to ask questions, to know which questions to ask, and when.

4 Removes fluff from the pipeline.

5 Improves forecasting accuracy.

6 Makes us better at negotiation.

7 Improves our close ratios.

8 Reduces gone dark scenarios (those where all communication has stopped).

To earn the right to ask questions, we must set our intentions and expectations for both parties immediately—within the first two minutes of a sales conversation. This allows us to respectfully say, "I am going to ask you questions, and you are going to ask me questions" without sounding silly or obnoxious.

Verbal Respect Contracts

Let's first dive into Verbal Respect Contracts (VRCs). There are different types of VRCs—there is one for a very first conversation, and others for different parts of business conversations throughout the sales funnel.

- **First Call VRC:** This happens in the first conversation you ever have with someone.

- **Second Call VRC:** When you have additional conversations and there are new people joining from the prospect's side.

- **Demo/Presentation VRC:** Generally, but not always, after a first call. It's used to clarify what's important to your prospect to see in the demo or take away from the presentation.

- **Negotiation VRC:** You should always have a conversation about the parameters of the negotiation conversation before you actually start it. Often used when speaking with procurement, CFO, or the final decision-maker on writing the check.

And there are more. You may have one for a pricing discussion, another for speaking with an IT or Security group, and another for an upsell or cross-sell opportunity. You may even have one for the unwinding of the relationship. And every department in the organization has a VRC they use for the different people they speak with as well, so Respect Contracts are not limited to just a sales or revenue organization.

Generally, a Verbal Respect Contract is broken down into six different sections. It could be more or fewer depending on the part of the sales cycle or which department is delivering it.

The primary elements are:

- Time
- Goals
- Agenda
- Potential Outcomes
- Social Contract
- Transition Statement

Here's an example of a VRC. This example is for a scheduled first qualification or discovery call for your account executive and new prospect who is interested in your services.

Hey Elyse,

Time: Thanks for making the time today (pause). I've got us down for thirty minutes—does that still work? Any hard stops I should be aware of? (pause) Great, at twenty-five minutes I will plan on calling a time-out so we can discuss next steps. By the way, if you see me looking down in the webcam view, it's me taking notes, and I will send them to you after this meeting. (pause)

Goals: Before we jump into things, I'd love to put some parameters around our discussion and any potential future discussions. (pause) Just so you know, my only goal for the call today is to establish a mutual frame of reference for us.

Agenda: I'd like to learn about your business and ask some questions. And of course, I'd love to share anything about what we do and answer your questions as well. (pause) Aside from the agenda I sent over, is there something specific you want to make sure we cover today?

Potential Outcomes: Just so you know, if at any point in this or a future conversation, you feel like we're not the right fit for you, please feel free to tell me. Likewise, if I discover something about your business that doesn't fit in our wheelhouse, I'll gladly tell you that. I will even go so far as to make recommendations for you based on what I learn from you. Is that fair? (pause)

Social Contract: Great. The last thing I'd want to do is bug you with "checking in," "reaching out," and "touching base" emails and calls that you hate getting and I hate making. (pause)

Transition Statement: What made you want to take this call today? What's happened internally that led us to chat?

Now you can see and get a feel for what this sounds like at the beginning of the relationship. The intention is to help our prospects and clients fall in trust with us and create the building blocks for an honest relationship that says, "Hey, we both respect each other's time, and if we're not a good fit, let's just walk away as friends."

At the conscious level, it immediately places both parties on a level playing field. A Respect Contract builds the foundation for a trusting relationship and helps lower the walls of resistance a prospect feels going into sales conversations. This is where they start to fall in trust with you.

Remember: *Customers will choose you based not just on what your business does, but more importantly on how you do business.*

Furthermore, the Respect Contract not only earns you the right to ask questions, it also gives you permission to take greater control of the entire sales process. Which then means you can ensure they have an amazing Buyer's Experience through your Seller's Journey.

Let's break down each section of the Respect Contract by examining the sample discussion above.

Time

Thanks for making the time today (pause). I've got us down for thirty minutes—does that still work? Any hard stops I should be aware of? (pause) Great, at twenty-five minutes I will plan on calling a time-out so we can discuss next steps. By the way, if you see me look down in the webcam view, it's me taking notes, and I will send them to you after this meeting. (pause)

What to Notice and Why It Works
"I've got us down for thirty minutes—does that still work?"

1 It confirms the time for both people.

2 It shows the prospect/customer that you are conscious they have a busy schedule too.

3 It tells your prospect that your time is of equal value to theirs and says, "Please respect my time like I am respecting yours, both in this conversation and in future conversations."

4 Essentially, you just asked for the next meeting within about fifteen seconds of meeting someone.

5 It makes sure there is enough time to actually have a wrap-up conversation so you don't end a meeting with the dreaded "doorknob blow-off" of "Hey, just email me next week and we can find a time."

6 I specifically call out my physical presence. Even though most of us know these things, we feel it's important to articulate them. This is another example of "how we do business."

Tip: yes, you can actually set an alarm for twenty-five minutes so you can move on to summarizing the conversation and asking for the next meeting.

All of this helps you earn the right to ask questions.

And equally important, simply acknowledging time begins to reduce the risk that prospects and customers sense in "having a sales call"—as well as your own anxiety about leading a sales call.

Essentially, it's a healthy exhale for all parties so we can begin to feel more comfortable.

In fact, you should be able to notice a change in voice, demeanor, and body language. It's like hitting the relax button.

Goals

Before we jump into things, I'd love to put some parameters around our discussion and any potential future discussions (pause). Just so you know, my only goal for the call today is to establish a mutual frame of reference for us.

Or:

Before we dive in, I wanted to say that I believe we are both here on a fact-finding mission. Let's exchange ideas and see if it makes sense to continue.

What to Notice and Why It Works

It's the plain truth. People appreciate honesty. Also:

1   It helps them relax and begin to open up even more.

2 It tells them you don't see this as a sales call at all; it's simply a conversation.

3 It tells them that this meeting is about both parties, not just you.

This is designed to help continually reduce the anxiety a prospect or customer may feel around talking to a salesperson, and to help the prospect further fall in trust with you the human, not you the salesperson. It also helps them begin to trust your stewardship through the Seller's Journey.

Agenda

I'd like to learn about your business and ask some questions. And of course, I'd love to share anything about what we do and answer your questions as well. (pause) Aside from the agenda I sent over, is there something specific you want to make sure we cover today?

What to Notice and Why It Works
It provides extreme focus on the conversation flow, and:

1 It allows the prospect or customer to add an item and gain a sense of control because they are approving the agenda.

2 It reduces the chances of tangent conversations from happening.

3 It provides a polite way to interrupt and get back on track if the tangent conversation does happen.

4 It allows us to take control from the prospect without them even being aware it's happening.

5 By setting this simple agenda and specifically mentioning you will ask them questions and they can ask you questions, you have officially #EarnedTheRight to ask any question you like.

Goals vs. Agenda

The Goals and Agenda sections sometimes get intertwined, which is fine.

Setting up the Goals portion of the Respect Contract is about making the end goal clear: what we want to accomplish by the end of this call, aka the Buyer's Experience.

The Agenda is all about how we're going to get there in *this* conversation—aka the Seller's Journey.

If your prospect has things they'd like to share or add to these sections, then you take the pauses, let them tell you, and take notes so you can always go back to those points when appropriate. Note that sometimes your prospect or buyer interprets this as the moment for them to start telling their story. This is actually a great signal—it means they are very engaged with you, and trusting you so much they are willing to start talking. And as we all know, when they start talking, it's hard to get them to stop.

Sometimes you will need to interrupt and stop them, and simply state, "Time-out—before we go there, I'd like to cover one or two things that won't take more than about thirty seconds."

Potential Outcomes

Just so you know, if at any point in this or a future conversation, you feel like we're not the right fit for you, please feel free to tell me. Likewise, if I discover something about your business that doesn't fit in our wheelhouse, I'll gladly tell you that. I will even go so far as to make recommendations for you based on what I learn from you. Is that fair?

What to Notice and Why It Works

Nothing will exhaust the spirit and will of a salesperson more than "chasing maybes." So it gives them the out you need to prevent this. In addition:

1 It shows ultimate confidence and competence. People like working with confident and competent people.

2 By telling them you will offer other solutions if you are not the right fit, it reduces their anxiety and again helps them fall in trust with you as a human and your organization as a whole.

3 It gives you a line in the sand for when they go dark or ghost you.

Setting the potential outcome is a huge piece to the "respect" portion of the contract. It's making the intention up-front that we don't want to waste one another's time—and that it's okay to walk away (and communicate it) if there isn't a good fit.

Again, it also shows your time is valuable and they should not waste your time any more than you want to waste theirs.

Doing this is going to help them stay in that Adult Ego state where they can make rational decisions and be honest about moving forward with you, or with someone else, ultimately preventing you from chasing maybes.

Just because they might be a CEO or a founder and you're a sales development rep (SDR) or account executive (AE) does *not* mean you have to give away confidence and power. Your time and hard work should be respected just as much as theirs, and that's what we want to get across in Potential Outcomes. It leads into the Social Contract.

And when someone goes dark or starts ghosting you, you'll have a clear way of dealing with it—we'll get to that in more detail below.

Social Contract

Great, the last thing I want to do is bug you with "checking in," "reaching out," and "touching base" emails and calls that you hate getting and I hate making. (pause)

What to Notice and Why It Works

It confirms you are both on the same page about how the sales process will work. Also:

1   It reinforces their commitment to your sales process.

2   When they agree, this also helps prevent them from ghosting you.

3   And if they do start ghosting you, and some will still do it, it allows for you to contact them very directly and specifically about where things stand without having to use the dreaded "reaching out," "checking in," "touching base," "circling back," "bubbling to the top," and all the other worthless phrases salespeople use.

The Social Contract is straightforward and allows you to connect emotionally to your prospects and customers. This is helpful because it will continually reduce the risk your prospects feel when working with you and encourage them to fall in trust with you.

Connecting emotionally with the other person on the line helps them understand where you're coming from. It's saying, "Hey, I really don't want to bother you after this call if you don't feel it's a fit or a priority, because we both know how frustrating that can be." Most likely, they've been in your shoes and will immediately agree. With your Respect Contract you've earned the right to move forward and dive into discovery.

There are different ways to tackle how you say this piece up-front, depending on if you're prospecting over email, through LinkedIn, holding calls on Zoom, and so forth, which we'll dive into a little bit later.

Transition Statement

What made you want to take this call today?

What's happened internally that led us to chat?

Now that we have gotten them to really fall in trust with us, we need to begin the discovery process.

Regardless of what someone has already shared, it's best to confirm what is driving them to even have a conversation. They may have already said things like:

- "We are in the market…"
- "We want to change vendors…"
- "We are curious about…"
- "My boss told me to research…"

Usually there is still something they haven't shared about what's actually happening in their organization that makes them curious, want to make a change, or made the boss ask for research.

This is the headache they have, and once we know this, we can help them determine if it's actually a migraine. And let's face it, everyone wants relief from a migraine, yes?

Here's a quick review. A Respect Contract:

1 Gives you the courage and confidence to establish and maintain control of the entire sales process.

2 Provides a guideline for you to maintain control in case the prospect takes you on tangents.

3 Formally gets them to agree to give you control.

4 Gets them to fall in trust with you.

5 Gives you a way to stay engaged professionally should they try to go dark on you.

6 Shows them you are very different from every other sales rep they have ever encountered.

Ghost Busting

Now let's talk about how using a Respect Contract actually helps you when someone goes dark or ghosts you.

The Respect Contract drew a line in the sand. It created a moment in space and time to which you can always refer back and hit the reset button.

You can do this in a voicemail, email, or LinkedIn message. Our preference is often email first.

Here is what it looks, sounds, and feels like:

Subject Line: Status Update Requested Please

Email Body:

Hey _____, when we first spoke, we both agreed if it was not a good fit we would let each other know.

When I go _____ weeks without hearing from someone, this is what it sometimes means.

Can you let me know if this is the case and you've decided to move in a different direction, or if you are just hitting pause for thirty days?

I have no desire to waste the space of your inbox if you are no longer interested.

I promise: telling me no will not hurt my feelings.

Sincerely,

[Rep Name]
[Phone]

What to Notice and Why It Works

It's specific to a time and agreement you both committed to, and:

1 It's professionally polite without being demanding.

2 You've #EarnedTheRight to ask this question.

3 It calls them out on their bullshit and encourages them to be truthful.

Of course, in reality some people simply will not respond. And while we don't like that, at least we can go to bed at night knowing we asked the question.

It also lays the framework for additional "breakup emails" to build upon this message should they not respond.

Doing It Right

To sum up: organizations do not choose to buy from you based on what your organization does. They buy based on the pains your product or service relieves *and* the Buyer's Experience, which is created by the Seller's Journey you have created. When you understand how and why a Respect Contract works, *and* you implement it as suggested, you will #EarnTheRight to ask questions, you will #EarnTheRight to be direct, and you will #EarnTheRight to walk away with your head held high because you did everything correctly.

A word of caution: if you shortcut any part of the Respect Contract, you will lose more deals, you will have more prospects ghost you, and your anxiety will consistently increase. Every single section of the Respect Contract is critical.

Yes, you can wordsmith it to sound authentic to your voice. However, that does not mean leaving out parts. Specifically, if you shortcut Potential Outcomes and do not specifically indicate they can walk away *and* you can walk away too, then your entire Respect Contract has failed. You will lose complete control of the entire sales process, and you will enter the Child Ego state—that place where fear and anxiety eat away at you because you are afraid to ask direct questions that get you honest answers. Even if they are answers you may not want to hear.

There are different types and ways of implementing Respect Contracts. All need to be thought through clearly and adjusted accordingly. In short, there are both digital and verbal Respect Contracts.

Three-Step Digital Respect Contracts

We are big believers in building respect in multiple ways. And we think you should not wait until the initial conversation to start doing that. Remember, people will purchase from you for two reasons: the pains you solve and how you do business. That is the focus of a Three-Step Digital Respect Contract. The primary examples are the calendar invite, LinkedIn, and a pre-meeting email.

Here is what we recommend to clients.

Step 1: Send Calendar Invite
- Copy all required parties
- Include Agenda
- Zoom/conference link
- Who is calling whom?
- It is OK to include your cell phone as "backup."

Step 2: Send a Pre-meeting Email
Subject Line:
- Include "Their Company/Your Company—Proposed Agenda"

Email Body:
- Polite and professional
- Future-minded with date included
- Ask if they want to add something to the agenda

Agenda:
- Item 1
- Item 2

Additional Info if Necessary:
- Links to specifically relevant information

Here's the actual email template we use:

Subject Line: Proposed Agenda: The Harris Consulting Group/Sales Training conversation with Richard Harris

Email Body:

Hey Bobby,

I look forward to speaking with you on _____. I wanted to put a few things front and center to help us make the most of your time. Feel free to add a topic as well.

Proposed Agenda
- Introductions
- Understand the State of the Harris Consulting Group Sales/Desires/Expectations
- Answer any questions about Richard/THCG
- Determine next steps, wider audience, etc.

COURSE AND SERVICES OVERVIEW—This will take 2 minutes to digest, and let us drive the conversation where you want.

One thing I ask everyone to think about is filling in the blanks to this question: "At the end of the engagement, we expect the team to be better at _____, _____, and _____.

What kinds of things fill in those blanks for you?

Thanks,

Richard

PS—You can schedule time on my calendar by CLICKING HERE

Step 3: Send LinkedIn Connection Request

Keep it simple:

> "Hey Richard, thought it would make sense to connect here. I look forward to speaking with you on [date]."

What to Notice and Why It Works

The subject line is clear, concise, and easy to find if they want to look for it again. Some other notes:

1 Include the actual date of the meeting in the first sentence.

2 Include the same agenda in both the email and calendar invite. Most people don't read the agenda in a calendar invite until it pops up five minutes before the meeting happens. And even then, maybe.

3 Proposed Agenda simply means they can ask for something specific.

4 The last question is designed to get them to start thinking about their headaches and migraines.

5 Yes, you send all three of the above message types. (If your prospects are not on LinkedIn, then skip it.)

6 It helps reduce no-shows—your prospect now has three items in their inbox reminding them of your meeting. No, they won't be annoyed.

{ 6 }

Listening and Asking Tactics

AS MANY PEOPLE SAY, "Failing to plan means you are planning to fail."

This means you need a map, and all maps have a few specific things:

1 **Title:** N.E.A.T. Selling

2 **Legend:** description, explanation, and other items to help with orientation

3 **Key:** a part of the legend that explains the symbols or gives scale

4 **Grid:** to help pinpoint your location

We have the title, the legend, and the key. We have our N.E.A.T. Selling compass helping us figure out directions. We have our understanding of how humans make decisions, we have a stronger sense of self with our Respect Contracts, and we have our process in place. Now we just need to know the specific moves we should make—the tactics we'll use to bring the humanity back into the selling process so that everyone wins.

These next few chapters and tactics are a part of your grid. They will help you complete your entire map of the Seller's Journey. And more specifically, they will help you pinpoint your location and determine how far away you are from your treasure.

How I view tactics in sales stems heavily from my own therapy experience. Sometimes you hear a new phrase or concept for the first time and it just sticks. It resonates so much that it becomes applicable to everything—and that's what happened to me when I really started diving into my own inner workings years ago.

When I learned about Transactional Analysis, I started thinking about how it relates to sales tactics. If Transactional Analysis talks about the communication exchanges between people, and tactics are the small actions we take to build trust between us and our potential customers, then it becomes clear how much we can interweave the two.

The first tactic, below, is the use of Active Listening.

Tactic 1: Active Listening

Without cheating, see if you can answer these questions:

Pop Quiz I: "The Piano Man" by Billy Joel.
- What was the old man drinking?
- Who was practicing politics?
- Who is the real estate novelist?

Pop Quiz II: "Single Ladies (Put a Ring on It)" by Beyoncé.
- How many years did she cry her tears?
- What kind of jeans is she wearing?
- What does she deserve?

Of course not everybody knows these songs, but they are songs people often sing along with. And yet when stopped to answer these questions, people often cannot remember the lyrics that specifically. The words are on the tip of their tongue but stop there.

Even when we're sure we're listening and sure we got what we heard, it doesn't always stick. So we have to be very present in conversations. And not only intentionally present, but curious and empathetic towards our prospects. We must open our minds to listening first, then thinking, and then, if the time is right, speaking. And sometimes we should not speak at all.

Active Listening is using your own internal and intentional being to fully listen and be present in the conversation, absorbing not just the words they are using but their tone of voice, mannerisms, and their overall presence. We do this by removing distractions, listening with our eyes, not just our ears, and slowing our breathing. It requires a true focus that is both intentional and purposeful. When we listen with intent and purpose, we are fully present, and that is a moment when a prospect or customer can begin to fall in trust with us.

Whenever I talk about this with teams, I make sure to stress the word "intent" because, let's be real, we all get distracted. We could be in the middle of a conversation and anxiously waiting to reply because we can't wait to answer their question or comment so that they know we're listening (the irony!). The practice is intentionally *listening*. Not anticipating a reply, not waiting to speak. Just listening with purpose.

That's the piece I always want teams to really understand: before you speak up, first make sure to tell yourself to focus, then speak.

When you're able to focus and actively listen, it allows you to operate on an equal basis with someone and meet them where they're at. Now, you might be thinking to yourself, "Yeah, okay, Richard. I do this all of the time. That's easy." Or maybe you're on the other side of the fence thinking, "Okay, but how exactly do I do that? What does it really *mean*?" Whichever one it may be, we're going to cover it all. Cue intention!

Removing Distractions

During the COVID pandemic, many of us were forced to move our work lives in with our home lives. Even since before the pandemic, we've been inundated with distractions thanks to social media. With all of these changes in our environments, I know I'm not the only one who's prone to distractions while on calls.

We feel a pressure to respond to every message, every person, every notification, every "ding." It's no surprise that with a day full of Zoom meetings, we can get completely distracted and stop being intentional in our conversations—which just makes it more necessary and important than ever before. The problem is, when people talk about Active Listening, it's rarely followed by advice on how to do it successfully.

So whenever I teach my clients about Active Listening, I start by talking through what we can remove physically from our environment to improve our listening.

If you're a pen chewer, a fidget spinner-er, or a 700-tab-opener... just get rid of it all. It may be tempting to keep something on your desk to play with while you're on calls. It might be extremely tempting to keep browser tabs open so you can try to sneak in an email or do a little extra research. We suggest going cold turkey and just cutting all of it. You may think these things help you, but in reality, they're just a crutch, and they're taking you away from the opportunity to really connect with your prospect.

If you like to keep your phone on your desk during calls, that's normal—but you're better off making sure it's silenced and put away. Just putting your phone face down is not removing the distraction; in fact, it's the opposite. It's saying the phone is more important than the audience; you just want to pretend it's not. The worst is being on a call and all of a sudden you have beeps and vibrations from Slack notifications, a text coming through, a LinkedIn message arriving... It's an easy way to make your prospect wonder if you're paying attention and a surefire way to signal that you're probably not. So your surroundings are just as important an Active Listening tactic as the listening itself.

So remove the distractions:

1 Calendar/Slack notifications off
2 Phone on silent and put behind you or in a drawer
3 Close all unnecessary computer tabs
4 No fidget spinners

Physically Being Present

Body language is everything, and it's a whole other sales skill to learn. (We won't go into the details here; you can buy whole books on it.) But when the pandemic hit, in-person meetings and coffee dates were nonexistent. We just had little screens to operate on with each other every day.

Sometimes you have to show someone you are listening, so what are some ways we can do this on a little screen? Maybe it's giving a head nod and an occasional "mm-hmm" so the other person knows you're listening and engaged. Maybe it's eye contact, smiling, eyebrows, or body posture.

The truth? It's a mix of all of the above. The challenge for salespeople is: do we notice these cues from the other person and use that knowledge to dig deeper and pause to ask more questions? Or do we just notice they're engaging in some capacity and move on? Take a second and think about a conversation you had recently and what you did. Did you pause and go deeper, or did you move on?

Here is our advice on confirming you are physically present for people, part of which we covered earlier in the Respect Contract.

First, explain your presence. Of course people know the camera, the screen, and the keyboard are in different places. And yes, we *hope* they are really paying attention to us. However, when I explain my video meeting setup, it also tells them they are very important and that nothing will distract me from our conversation. A plus to doing this is that it reminds them to be more present as well.

Second is note-taking. When your prospect knows you are taking notes, they know you are listening. And we go one step further: we explain the notes we take. Here's the template we use to take notes for client calls. Feel free to use it as well.

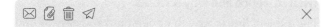

Subject Line: Prospect Company/Your Company:
Next Steps/Call Notes/Commercial Terms

Hey [Contact]

Great speaking with you today. Please use this email as a summary of our conversation. Would you please respond and let me know if I captured everything correctly?

Next Steps
- Richard to include
- [Contact] to speak to the internal team
- Richard and [Contact] to speak again [date]

Challenges & Training
- At the end of the engagement, we expect the team to be better at _____, _____, and _____.

Timeline
- [Company] needs to complete the project by [date]

Commercial Terms
- $$$$$$

Thanks,

[Rep Name]
[Phone]

What to Notice and Why It Works

The subject line is easy to understand and easy to find. Also:

1 The second sentence is critical. If they don't respond, they now have skin in the game if something is off.

2 Next steps are immediate. That's always the most important thing.

3 It is purposely written to look short so people will scroll through. Even if they hate long emails, it's OK; it shows I am detail-oriented.

4 It's written in such a way that they can forward the email to others on their team.

5 It shows them I am actively listening.

6 It gets them to further fall in trust with us based on how we do business, not just the pains we solve.

Tactic 2: Empathy

Active Listening and empathy go hand in hand. It is almost impossible to be empathetic towards someone if we are not doing a good job of listening with intent.

The definitions of empathy we like to refer to are from professor and author Brené Brown. She argues that empathy is about fueling a connection between two people. It is not sympathy. As she describes it, sympathy drives a disconnection.

Empathy helps people feel included. When we say things like "You are not alone" and we mean it, that connects people. Empathy is about being committed to fully understanding someone's experience. It requires a conscious effort of perspective-taking.

So, when we do a good job of actively listening, it means we can truly meet our prospects and customers in their headspace. It means we are able to understand their perspective; we can hopefully not be judgmental about them and their experiences, we can comprehend the emotions they are feeling, and of course we can articulate this recognition to them. And if we are really good, we can be vulnerable and ask them to confirm if we are interpreting and understanding things correctly.

All of which goes back to the principles of Active Listening.

Note: we feel the need to separate Active Listening and empathy as two different tactics. They are often used as buzzwords, but rarely explained in a business setting.

After all, it's possible to actively listen and not feel or demonstrate empathy. At least that's what my family sometimes says to me.

Tactic 3: Open- and Closed-Ended Questions

We've earned the right to ask questions with a Respect Contract. We know there are two kinds of questions: open-ended and closed-ended. We also know the difference—or do we? And we've been taught that open-ended questions are better—but are they always?

Here are a few things to know about open- and closed-ended questions.

Advantages of Open-Ended Questions

The best thing about open-ended questions is that they force us to shut up. It's not that we don't get a yes or no answer; it's that they require us, the salespeople, to be quiet and actively listen.

1   They give us time for strategic thinking. While listening, we get a moment to strategize on where to guide the conversation next.

2   They give our prospects just the right amount of control. In fact, in some cases they may feel they are in control. *Hint: they are not.*

3 They help our prospects hear themselves admit their own problems. When they hear it in their own words, it has deeper meaning.

4 They help our prospects and customers engage their Child Ego state. Remember, the Child Ego is the one that says, "*I want it!*"—including customers wanting to solve their problems.

Advantages of Closed-Ended Questions

There are definitely moments when closed-ended questions are helpful in the sales process. A properly timed closed-ended question forces the rational mindset or Adult Ego in an attempt to get an answer about moving forward. Remember, the Adult Ego gives us permission to move forward.

This is what the process may look like:

1 Salesperson asks, "So, based on this, can I send the contract over?"

2 Prospect quickly thinks in the following way:

- **Child Ego:** How much do I want to solve this problem?

- **Parent Ego:** Is this the right or wrong solution? Is it the appropriate time to move forward?

- **Adult Ego:** What are the downsides or upsides of moving forward right now?

3 Prospect gives a yes or no answer.

Tactic 4: And vs. But

"And" and "but" are two of the simplest words in the English language, and yet they are often misunderstood and misused in sales.

Consider these examples:

I understand what you are saying, *but*...

I understand what you are saying, *and* I wonder how you would feel about...

I agree with you, *but*...

I agree with you, *and* what if...

Do you see what's going on?

"And" introduces an additional idea and probes for further explanation. "But" contradicts what was previously said and dismisses the other person's idea, which can then be interpreted as a rejection of their emotions. Ever had to break up with someone? Or has someone broken up with you? That's the stronger version of the same emotion you trigger when you use the word "but."

In short, the word "but" dismisses everything that was said before it; the word "and" allows you to simply acknowledge what was said and subconsciously tells the other party you agree with them, even if you do not. It's much easier to get someone to change their mind when they feel you agree with them. Using "and" allows for this to happen.

Now, there are two parts of this to consider when putting it into practice.

One: actively listen to your prospects and listen for when they use the word "but." What happens when you hear them use it? Are they pretending to agree with you?

Two: try to be conscious of when you use the word "but"; see if you can flip it into an "and." This takes some time to get used to, and don't worry if you do not always get it right, but try it and see if you feel like it can work for you.

(Incidentally, I use the word "but" 88 times in this book, including the 10 times I used it just to talk about it in this tactic. I use the word "and" 1,087 times in the book. *And* yes, that was intentional.)

Tactic 5: Bucketing Discovery Questions

One of the simplest techniques we recommend for all clients is to "bucket" discovery questions—that is, draft them in advance and sort them into categories.

For example, if you are going to try to determine Access to Authority, what are the questions you could use? If you are going to drive to Economic Impact, what are the questions to use for that? In many cases a lot of the questions will be the same, and of course, with each new prospect or client, you will want to make some adjustments as needed. You saw some of this above in the list of questions to have ready for each part of N.E.A.T. Selling. We want to encourage people to practice this at much more specific levels. Think specific use cases in the sales process. In these examples we are often doing a different kind of discovery.

Often discovery is thought to refer to the prospect's or customer's specific pains. That is not always the case. We have to do discovery throughout the sales process. And it is important to have a few buckets of questions for your unique situations.

We often teach this bucketing technique as a "pre-qualifying" moment before providing something of value to your prospects and customers. So often we are eager to simply give the demo or send the proposal, and we forget to do some discovery there.

Here is how you use the bucketing technique to pre-qualify. Before a demo, make sure you ask and get clear answers to the following questions:

1   What are the three things you want to make sure you review through this demo?

2   After demos like this, our most successful customers take the information back to their team for review. Normally, when you do that, who would be the most skeptical person on the team?

3   What would the most skeptical person want to see if they were here today?

4   After I show you this demo, and you take it to your team, and if your team is still interested, what happens from your side as a next step?

Before sending a proposal, make sure you ask and get clear answers to the following questions:

1   When could we schedule some time to walk through the proposal?

2   How long does it normally take for a proposal to be finalized?

3   Once we review the proposal, what will happen next on your side?

4   How many approvals does the proposal have to go through?

5 Who else sees it after you?

6 What other departments have to sign off on the proposal even though they have given the verbal go-ahead?

7 Is anyone going to be on PTO during this process that we should think about now?

8 What is the one thing that would prevent this proposal from going forward to contracting?

Objection and Competition Tactics

WE ALL KNOW THAT a sales conversation is not just easy talk and easy questions and answers, and that it doesn't always move smoothly through discovery and qualifying and on towards closing. Even if you never say "but," your customer probably will. So our next tactics are for what to do about these points of friction and opposition.

Tactic 6: Don't Handle Objections, Marinate in Them

Pretty please, with sugar on top, stop "handling" customer objections!

I mean, who here wants to be "handled"?

In fact, we think you should *love* objections! Objections are the best purchasing signals *ever*!

That does not mean they're signals that someone will purchase. They are signals that someone is *interested* in purchasing. And they are telling you some of the primary obstacles you will need to get through to make this a real opportunity and a real deal.

As Michael Rosen writes in *We're Going on a Bear Hunt*, "We can't go over it, we can't go under it, we've got to go through it!"

And the only way to "go through" something is to marinate in it for a while.

Yes, it will be uncomfortable at first, and then you do it and it becomes easier. And then you do it again, and it becomes a bit easier still, and so on. And then you really start to love marinating in objections.

I believe these are the wins that feel better than getting the signature. The signature is a relief, but marinating in objections, those are the wins. For me, it's where the hardest of the hard work is done and won.

There is probably a "Big Book of Objections" or "Battle Cards" somewhere in your organization. Sometimes it's an actual asset on a shared drive, sometimes it's just folklore passed from generation to generation. Sometimes it's written by marketing, sometimes by sales, and the best ones are when sales and marketing work together on them.

The most common objections—errr, buying signals—typically include:

- Competitor
- ROI (return on investment)
- Budget
- Procurement
- Legal Redlines
- The Committee
- The Boss Said "No"
- Build vs. Buy
- Do Nothing

Now, we do need scripts for each of these scenarios; however, every one of these objections is really just a smoke screen. What is behind 99 percent of these objections is our inability to show the real value, the Economic Impact, of our solution to their problems.

Before getting into how to marinate in them, let's first address a mindset we often experience, and then we can provide clear and specific examples. It all comes down to one word: "fear." We call it one of the f-bombs of sales.

Fear is an unpleasant, often strong emotion caused by anticipation or awareness of danger or threat with an anticipated outcome of loss. In sales, and life. And in sales, it is specifically a fear of rejection.

So what happens when we hear these objections? And more importantly, how does it make us feel when we hear them? So often there is a real fear. Fear of loss, of rejection, of having to tell our boss. And all of this is wrapped in a big blanket of disappointment. Disappointing our boss, maybe disappointing our partner. And often disappointing ourselves.

So, let's marinate here for a moment.

When we hear or even perceive the word "no," some studies indicate the brain releases chemicals that immediately interrupt its normal functioning, impairing logic, reason, language processing, and communication. In short, perhaps inducing some level of panic. When we hear "no," fight-or-flight chemicals are released in our brain. And when we are in that mindset, it's hard for us to think rationally. Remember that analogy about breaking up with someone. When someone broke your heart, how easily were you able to *get over it*? Were you able to think clearly and rationally?

So when your prospect brings up the competition, it often feels like that "let's just be friends" breakup.

And we want to just get out of the conversation as quickly as we can, but sadly, we end up fumbling our way through it. We start marinating in the competition.

We ask you to marinate in these thoughts here because we want you to know it's normal and nobody is immune. Not you, not me, not your sales leaders, mentors, or customers.

You can even go deeper if you like. Sometimes the emotion behind that fear is jealousy. Jealousy of losing the deal to the competitor. And sometimes that fear is really masking anger. Anger that your leadership team is asking you to do "one more thing" that is ridiculous.

By surfacing these emotions, we can work to acknowledge them as real, accept them as they are, and learn to work through them in a different way with a different outcome.

Now, with life comes experience and wisdom, and we can use this wisdom to create a little bit of room in our own headspace to acknowledge the emotion we are feeling, and then we are able to use our adaptive skills to move forward with a little less anxiety. I have no desire that you become an expert at all of this simply by reading a book. I only want you to be aware that it is OK to acknowledge the emotions you are feeling. And generally speaking, when we acknowledge them, we can move towards something we prefer.

Here is an example. Someone tells you they like a certain feature of your competitor. And so often our initial reaction is to bring out the Big Book of Objections we were taught and go through the bullet points. And sadly it often sounds to the customer like, "Yeah, but..." While unintentional, it sounds dismissive and combative to our prospects and customers. This is us "handling the objections."

So what would marinating in it sound like? Instead of trying to refute the objection, jump in the pool and swim around with it. Maybe ask some additional questions:

- Yes, I've heard that is very cool. Specifically what do you like about it so much?

- We understand. I am curious: how does this solve your problem in relation to our solution?

- Do you feel it's a better look or actually easier to use than our solution?

- Understanding you like this feature of theirs, how important is this one feature to you in making this decision?

And what the most successful reps who have taken our training do is, the moment they hear an objection, they go into question mode to ask more about the objection rather than spewing what was given to them on their competitor battle card.

All of this ties in with what we discussed above: ego states, Active Listening, empathy. This is where your map all starts to make more sense.

And yes, you can do everything exactly as I suggest in this book, and you will still lose deals. I do too. But I believe it's better to lose with your head held high and giving it everything you've got, saying everything you can to focus on the win, than win by doing something silly or stupid (aggressive discounting) and then feeling dirty or guilty about it. That feeling often sounds like "Ugh, I hate that we had to discount" or "Pfftt... we are better than the competition, we should not have caved so much on pricing."

So let's marinate in the competition a little.

Tactic 7: The Competition

The truth shall set you free, but it may sting at first.

Let's first define the competition in a sales world and specifically how your prospect or customer views it. All too often we hear the word "competition" and think of an external vendor like us. However, the competition comes in many flavors. Sometimes it is another vendor they are considering. Other times it's the build vs. buy that a company thinks is less expensive: they think it is cheaper to build something themselves than to pay an outside vendor. In some cases they think they can build it at 80 percent of what you can do and still think that is a win. Then there is the "do nothing" decision, which is actually a competitor in its own right.

And of course there are competing priorities internally from other departments. There is only so much money to go around, so you may not lose to your direct competitor; you may lose to some other project or department in the organization you didn't even know exists. Sometimes those priorities are out of the control of our primary contact. And this is exactly what happens when you think about Access to Authority and all the different committees your product or service has to go through.

For now, let's focus on the traditional competitor: your business rival, the archenemy. You know the one—as soon as you hear it mentioned your heart sinks, or you *pray* your prospects and customers don't know much about it just yet.

Whenever you are in a competitive situation, you must always be 100 percent truthful. The easiest way to tell when a salesperson is not being truthful when discussing the competition is how they answer competitive questions with a bunch of "umms" and "ahhs." If you've practiced reducing these, which one can do, the other way to tell is when there is an overabundance of confidence. It comes off as dismissive to the prospect.

So, if you slow down your pace, lower your voice, and ask some questions that show you are actively listening, this is the first indication to your prospect that you are telling the truth. And then this is reinforced by what you explain specifically as your ability to "Yes we can" or "No we cannot," not simply a workaround solution that sounds wishy-washy with umms and uhhs.

With this in mind, at what price are you, as a customer, ever willing to make a purchasing decision without seeking advice from anyone or anything? "Anyone" would be a friend, a significant other, a boss, or a committee in your organization. "Anything" would include the internet or the "other brand" you see on the shelf in the store.

The answer is always $0.

As humans we are comparison shoppers, period. It does not matter what it is. The moment we see a price we have an emotional reaction, and then we compare that purchasing option against something else.

Picture someone buying a pack of gum at the checkout line. People are always comparing that to something—a different flavor, perhaps mints instead of gum, maybe that candy bar? And in some cases, they are comparing it to buying nothing. That is a comparison too: "no decision" is still a decision.

In addition, we are "envy" shoppers. At some point in our lives, we have made decisions like least expensive vs. most expensive. Sometimes the least expensive pasta is OK for you, but if you are entertaining others, perhaps you are going to splurge. And why do we splurge? Because we don't want to look bad to our guests. We are comparing ourselves to their perceptions of us.

Now, think about a purchase of $500, $10,000, or $100,000. Do you really think your prospects are not going to shop around? And yet one of the most common and perhaps dumbest things ever taught in sales is "Don't ever bring up the competition, because we don't want them to go shop around."

I bought into this stupidity as both a rep and a manager. If you have too, I've got some news for you: they're already shopping around. In those moments when you believe they have not spoken to someone else, you have two choices:

1   Be an ostrich and keep your head in the sand and pretend and pray they do not shop around.

2   Ask them about the competition, feeling confident that they will still choose you.

If you choose #1, I suggest you do some shopping around of your own, namely for a drug called "hope-i-um," because you'll really need it pretty soon.

If you truly see yourself as a value seller or trusted advisor, then you have to address the topic of the competition. It's also easier to discuss when you bring it up first. And here is why: when your prospect asks you first about the competition, it will put you in an emotionally defensive (Child Ego) state. This is a position of weakness. But if you bring it up first, then who will be feeling defensive?

And on top of that, they'll feel like they got caught with their hand in the cookie jar. And sometimes they will feel guilty. In this moment, as a trusted advisor, you become the Nurturing Parent, letting them know it's OK and helping them make the best decision for them.

When you do this right, they will choose you because you are the trusted advisor. And when you do it and they still choose someone else, you will be better equipped to get real answers on why they chose someone else instead of you. And they will walk away with a very positive impression of you that will put great karma into the sales universe, which will come back tenfold for you in the future, either with them or someone else.

Or you can ignore what I am suggesting and keep smoking your hope-i-um.

Remember: when engaging competition questions, we should always be 100 percent honest. One. Hundred. Percent. We will address the "Don't talk bad about your competitors" approach in a moment. For now, just know you should always be truthful.

Example 1: Bringing Up the Competition First

Generally speaking, I suggest bringing up the competition in the very first call.

If they have already shopped around or even spoken to a competitor, it is imperative that we know what they like and dislike about your rival. Otherwise we could completely miss something they see as extremely relevant to making the decision.

Here is the Indirect Approach:

- As you look to solve this problem, where did you hear about us?

- As you look to solve this problem, what else have you seen in the marketplace?

  - Great, what did you like about those solutions?

  - What did you dislike about them?

  - How important are _____ and _____ to you making these decisions?

These questions allow you to go fishing for information. And if you get a nibble or a bite, you can then go deeper to understand where to spend your time with them—making sure you share the items that are most important to them regarding your solution, and not spending time on the things you *think* they want to hear about.

Now, if you do not get a nibble, then it's time to go direct. And in some cases you can simply go direct from the get-go. It's more of a personality preference of the sales rep on which way to go.

Here's the Direct Approach:

- Who else have you spoken with about solving this problem?

- What other companies have you talked to so far?

- Who else will you be speaking with besides us?

Being direct, honest, and up-front will help keep you from being blindsided later, and in many cases it will allow you to truly understand the viability of the opportunity.

And we recommend supplementing the Direct Approach with the same follow-up questions from the Indirect Approach:

- Great, what did you like about those solutions?

- What did you dislike about them?

- How important are _____ and _____ to you making these decisions?

Example 2: Competitive Feature

So you're in a conversation and your prospect brings up the competitor. Specifically, they bring up a feature that you may not yet have. Before you can say anything, you feel those fight-or-flight chemicals being released like water from behind a dam. They start to flood your brain, creating a fog and a sense of panic.

And then you remember the "battle card" and what we are supposed to say to "handle this objection." It often sounds like this: "Here's our workaround."

Well, you may need to say that; however, I believe you need to marinate in this topic just a bit more. Not much, just a few sentences. It could sound something like this:

Hey _____ ,

Yes, we've heard great things about that feature. I am curious:

How important is that feature to you in making the decision?

What specific pains does it solve for you?

When you compare this feature to the things we can do that they cannot, which will be the most important to you?

Now, you may not ask all of these questions. If I could only ask one of them, it would be "How important is that feature to you in making the decision?"

The reason why is simple. We often think the competitor feature that someone brings up is a must-have; after all, why else would they bring it up? This is just something we assume.

You would be surprised how often it's actually not that important. The reason they are asking is because they are in comparison mode—they need to compare you to the competitor, and it's all they can think of in that particular moment.

Now, on the flip side, let's say it *is* really important to the decision. While you may not want to hear that, I'd much rather know the reason I lost a deal, which means I need to ask. I would much rather know the real answer instead of relying on guesswork and wondering why they went dark on me.

And let's take that one step further.

How much time would you spend mourning the lost deal if you knew the real answer was a specific competitive feature vs. not knowing the answer at all? For me, when I know the reason why someone went in a different direction, I can let go of it and stop thinking about it a lot sooner. When I don't know the answer, I can spend hours, days, even months being sad, angry, and yeah, even depressed about it. Simply because all I am left with is the dreaded "It's not you, it's me" breakup.

Example 3: General Competitive Comparison

This approach is recommended for when you are going head-to-head with a competitor. Sometimes it is during a net new sales conversation, and other times it's when you are working to displace the incumbent.

You are in a conversation and your prospect asks, "So, how do you compare yourself to competitor __?" Do you start bad-mouthing them in some stupid tirade? Of course not. Do you start launching into nasty rumors? Of course not.

Now consider this.

1 Have you ever won a deal against your competition?

2 Have you ever had someone come back to you after they went with your competitor and had a bad experience?

3 Have you ever gone after your competitor's clients and won?

Well, what I am about to suggest is not speaking poorly about your competitor at all. Because it's based in fact, not opinion.

It goes something like this:

Hey _____,

I understand you are considering competitor _____ and I am wondering: would you be open to hearing what our most successful clients have told us about why they chose us over them?

Or:

I understand you are considering competitor _____ and I am wondering: would you be open to hearing what our most successful clients have told us about why they *moved from* them to us?

Well, our most successful clients have told us they chose us because of _____. How important is this to you?

So, what is the most interesting part of this? Some think it's that you are using a customer story to share the truth, and therefore you are not disparaging the client, you are simply sharing information. That's a piece of it, but there is actually something better.

The most important part is using this phrase: "our most successful clients."

What does everyone want to be? They want to be the "most successful." Nobody in business wants to be mediocre.

If you do your job properly, you will help your prospects realize they don't have headaches; they have migraines. Nobody wants to suffer from a migraine, and you, as the trusted advisor, are required to help them relieve it.

And the other cool part of this technique is specifically using the word "and" in these conversations.

So often when we get in competitive situations, we use the word "but." "I understand you like them, but..." or "But don't you want to hear about..."

As you may recall, "but" is dismissive of the other person's emotional belief systems. Using "and" acknowledges their emotions and belief systems as real, and because you earned the right to share this information with them, they are willing to hear a non-combative alternative. And (see, did it again) they actually opened the door for you to walk right in.

{ 8 }

Money, Pricing, and Commercial Terms Tactics

THE NEXT POINTS OF friction come when you're talking money. Even if you have the best product for their needs and you both know it, they will probably try to pay less than you're asking. It may not even be a real budgetary constraint for them. They may just want the "win."

You can't just wait for these objections to land. You need to be proactive. And you need to understand the different types of money conversations.

Tactic 8: The ROI Conversation (Mindset)

The dumbest thing ever uttered by anyone making a purchase is questioning the return on investment (ROI). It can be anything like the following:

- Do you have any data around the ROI of your product or service?

- My boss (CFO) is going to ask about the ROI; what can I share with them?

- Can you prove to me your ROI?

So listen up, buttercups, I am looking at your C-level exec who loves to manage through spreadsheets and never had to worry about their job because they didn't ever have to carry the bag.

The jig is up!

Here is why you asking about ROI helps me know you are not as smart about negotiating as me. I know, and everyone knows—at least they do now—that no matter what I tell you, you will not believe me. Marie Curie, Steve Jobs, and Stephen Hawking could all be resurrected tomorrow, get a billion dollars in funding to create an ROI calculator, and you still would want them to show their work like a fifth-grade math teacher.

What this tells me is that you are lying. You are saying this because the moment I say, "So when I show you the ROI, you are ready to sign, right?" you will have another excuse.

And do you know who the easiest people to negotiate with are? Liars. Because one lie begets the next, and the next thing you know the liar just tangled themselves up in a spiderweb of their own design. If you think I am wrong, ask any parent how easy it is to tell when their kids are lying to them and how they get them to confess. It's the same skill. Just a different spoiled child.

Now, the real challenge is for the seller. It's about us. It's about whether we've done a good job determining Economic Impact through better discovery. Did we ask the right questions to get our prospects and customers to give us real numbers that prove Economic Impact?

And even if we did and the numbers make sense regardless of budget, are we or our bosses willing to walk away? If not, you will lose every time.

So here are some tactics you can use around pricing to help you get through the dumbest things your prospects and customers will bring up.

Tactic 9: Commercial Terms

Improving negotiation skills is one of the most frequent requests we get when it comes to sales training. When I dig deeper, though, our customers finally realize it's not the negotiation skills that need improving; it's that the team's discovery skills simply suck.

If a salesperson cannot get the prospect to articulate the Economic Impact of the pains they are experiencing, there is no way they are ready to handle pricing and negotiation conversations. And you will fall into the ROI trap.

So let's start with some basics: pricing and budget vs. Commercial Terms.

Anytime a prospect starts using the words "pricing" or "budget," especially early in the conversation, we immediately change that phrase to "Commercial Terms." And here is why: commoditization.

People naturally shop by comparison. This means your customers come in with a specific frame of reference and treat every purchase like a commodity. And in their mind, you are always just like the least expensive version of something and therefore you have less value. Then as the customer digs in more, they must start selling themselves on the superior quality of one item over the next.

The simplest example is purchasing cars. Generally speaking, we know there is a pricing difference between a Ferrari and a Hyundai. We also know that we cannot walk into a Ferrari dealership and demand a Hyundai price simply because they both have four wheels and get us from one place to the next.

However, your buyer does not see it this way. In many cases, they do not even understand their own pains and what those pains are costing them in real dollars, and therefore they want Ferrari performance at a Hyundai price. (And by the way, this is not a slight on Hyundai; it's simply an example.)

So when our prospects come to us, they are naturally thinking lowest price and highest performance. That's OK, we all do it. And because they so often come with an anti-salesperson bias, they also want to *win* against the salesperson.

It's our job to help them feel the difference between us and everyone else. We want them to want us (an example of the Child Ego state).

Once they do, that's when we know we are closer to an actual deal. And this is achieved by changing the conversation in various parts of the sales cycle. One way to do that is to start early and speak to their consciousness, which can eventually shift their subconscious biases.

For example, you are on the first call with a prospect and they inevitably ask, "How much does it cost?"
And reps get very nervous and start stumbling around
with "Well, uhh, it depends on..." or "Well, I can
ballpark it..."

Just like the ROI conversation, this is your biggest
moment of weakness. You have just told your buyer
there is no fixed price, and the way you said it suggests
you are scared. They are sharks, and they smell your
blood in the water. And they are very hungry.

So if we shift our answer ever so slightly, we can
establish more value and credibility.

The sooner we start using the phrase "Commercial
Terms," the sooner we lay a new foundation in both
their conscious and subconscious mindsets. A foundation that says this will be about an exchange of goods
and services for a certain amount of money that's fair
for all parties.

It reminds them there is real value to what they are
purchasing, and neither you nor your company are a
commodity. It means your competition is just treating
your prospect like the prospect has a headache. "Commercial Terms" helps the prospect understand they
actually have a migraine. And we can empathize with
them and help them take this pain away.

Remember, people choose to work with you not
just because of what you do or the price you set. How

you conduct business factors in. Elevating the conversation around money shows you see and understand their big picture, their specific pains, and that you both understand things need to be fair.

Tactic 10: How Does That Feel?

Anytime I see a price that is an even number in something like B2B software and hardware sales—$10,000, $25,000, $100,000—I already know this is just someone picking some number. Hopefully they have done their research and the price is in line with the market rate, but even if that is the case, I already know I can start to negotiate. Someone on their team doesn't understand how to use the distraction of odd numbers to reduce discounting.

Ever wonder why when you choose font sizes they are always even numbers? It's simple. It's because they are easy to digest. There is no complexity, so your mind does not have to think very hard. It's just an easy solution and it's been provided to you.

On the flip side, odd numbers make you pause and think, just for a microsecond.

Ever adjusted that font size from an even to an odd number? Did you go from 14 to 16, then realize you had to use 15? And sometimes that still "feels weird."

Even something as simple as $7.99 makes us pause and think, oh, that's $8, not $7. For that microsecond we are distracted.

So when quoting prices to our prospects, we should do the same thing: use odd numbers so we can cause a distraction. Because the next four words are the most important words you will ever use in your negotiations: "How does that feel?"

For example, "So the cost of our services is $15,479. How does that feel?"

Your prospect hears this number and because it's so random they are trying to figure out what you just said, or how you even came up with such a bizarre number. They cannot even round this number to $15,500 very easily. This is the distraction.

As discussed earlier, every time people see a price they have an emotional response to it. Their *feelings* take over, and your prospect cannot resist sharing them with you.

Here are the responses we hear:

1 Oh, that's higher than we were expecting.
2 Oh, that feels about right.
3 Oh, that's less than we were expecting.

We can then start the negotiation process as needed, based on the answer. Even the most sophisticated

CFOs cannot resist an honest answer and lower their defenses when it comes to negotiating.

Of course many CFOs are going to say it's "too expensive" or "more than we have budgeted"; however, they are still so distracted thinking about this bizarro odd number that they don't even realize their emotional defense mechanism and negotiation skills have opened the door for me to maintain pricing integrity.

And here's one thing we notice and of course love: that old-school CFO who loves to scare salespeople. Oftentimes they are so distracted by the odd number, they give a purely emotional response and never use the word "budget." They are simply too distracted.

So why does this happen? Because nobody has prepped or trained them how to avoid answering this question without being honest. You will hear it in their tone of voice. It will shift. It will not be as strong as the standard "Oh, it's outside our budget." They may say those words, but they will not have the annoying paper-cut feel you often experience when you hear it.

You will see them squirm and see their eyes and eyebrows shift uncontrollably. These are their "tells." And this is the moment you win.

Remember, pricing doesn't have a look or a sound. It is a *feeling*, always.

Now, what happens if you ask "how does that feel?" and you still get "that looks high" or "that sounds too expensive"?

What is really happening is they are having an emotional response. We want them to tell us how it feels because when they do, we can have a real conversation about Commercial Terms.

Tactic 11: Handling the Discount

Are you really shocked by the discount question? I mean really?

If you are, then you must either be new in sales or constantly smoking the hope-i-um.

Please stop discounting at high levels like 30 percent, or even 20 or 10. You are hurting yourself and falling into the "fear of loss" trap. Or better yet, simply stop discounting altogether.

By the way, do you present the discount as "hey, I am doing you a favor" when you bring it to your prospect? News flash: they don't see it that way. They see it as "we are doing you a favor allowing you to sell to us."

In addition, you are setting yourself up for greater disappointment, anger, and frustration next year at renewal time. That's when you get the "grandfather pricing" conversations with customers who expect to pay the same amount every year.

So what happens because of the discount you gave in the first contract?

1 Your leadership is angry at you, especially since they approved the price last year.

2 Your customer thinks they are doing you a favor.

3 Your Customer Success team is already behind the eight ball on the first day the contract comes up for renewal.

4 Your customer is going to be angry at you in a year when you give them the higher price because they think they have been doing you a favor, not the other way around.

5 Your leadership team is angry at you again because they think you cannot do your job and raise the price.

So whose fault is all of this anger resulting from discounting? Your CEO's. Ultimately, they are the person who allows for a discounting culture. Even if they are not aware of it, they are, because in the board meeting "the buck stops with them." Your leadership team did a shitty job on product/market fit and pricing if your organization is always discounting.

There are many times you can charge more than your competitor. Remember, it all goes back to the Buyer's Experience, having them fall in trust with you, helping them explain their migraines, and Economic Impact.

Sure, I can fly somewhere more cheaply on Southwest Airlines than Delta, usually. Yet Delta still sells those seats at a higher price. So you don't have to discount as much as you probably do, and in some cases you may not have to discount at all.

Now, sometimes discounting is unavoidable for one reason or another. If you must discount, here is what we have done in the past and teach our clients. When someone asks for a discount, and assuming you will negotiate, simply say the following:

There are four ways we can both leverage commercial terms:

1 Marketing support (case study, logos, customer quotes)
2 Multiyear contracts
3 Prepayment
4 Additional licenses

Which ones would you like to discuss?

Everyone thinks discounts need to be big. We recommend making each of these discounts small to start and letting them scale. So if they choose one, they get a 2.59 percent discount; if they choose all four, they get a 9.17 percent discount. Yes, this is just under 10 percent, and that is on purpose.

Once you start discounting, you have two options:

1 You can say that's all there is.
2 You can negotiate a bigger discount.

If you're negotiating the bigger discount, remember: the prospect wants a big win, and that win is as much emotional as it is financial.

Now imagine you have to give up more. We suggest 15 percent as your ceiling. And here's why. From the prospect's perspective, they nearly doubled the discount (from 9.17 percent), therefore they "won," and most importantly, they feel they were "better at negotiating" than the salesperson.

OK, let them have that win in their mind. But remember that discounting hurts you in the future. So what do you do to help prevent that awkward moment in nine or ten months when it's time to renew?

If you discount the first contract, please be sure it is specifically stated in all your communications that it is the "first year only." And it is imperative that in the contract there is phrasing such as "Upon renewal, the pricing will be adjusted to standard market rates."

Failure to do this will simply make renewals that much harder and frustrate you, your Customer Success team, your boss, your executive team—and your customer.

Here's a hint: go to your leadership team, legal team, or whoever controls the contract template and tell them they have to figure out the right wording. And if they cannot or will not, then you have an indication on the leadership sales skillset. Make note of this—it will matter as you make career decisions.

As your deal sizes get bigger and the companies you sell into also become larger, one of the final steps in the negotiation process is dealing with procurement. In some cases you may not ever be able to speak with someone on the procurement team; in others you most certainly will. This section is dedicated to the best practices on how to approach a conversation with procurement—one that is not always about price.

When you get to procurement, it is important to think of them as a new customer, not just another department you need to get through to get the deal signed. And like all customers, they have specific needs. So it is your job to do discovery on those needs.

Remember: their job is to save the company money, and it's not wrong—but that is not their only motivation or initiative.

Tactic 12: Negotiating with Procurement

The most important thing to know about procurement is that they are not your enemy. I know this may be shocking for some, but after speaking with several leading Fortune 500 companies' procurement representatives, I've found they are actually on our side.

Now, this does not mean they are going to simply pay what is asked. It really means they get it. They know how salespeople are compensated.

Here are some things you might not know about procurement departments:

1 Their job is to analyze the options and help the company make good decisions. This does not always mean it has to be the lowest price.

2 Sometimes savings can mean not increasing costs. Sometimes it means they understand the long tail of a total cost savings in relation to cash flow.

3 They do not want pricing conversations to be adversarial.

4 They don't feel that discounts have to be 20 percent, 30 percent, 40 percent all the time.

5 They actually want to hear from sales sooner than later. Yes, this means they want to be involved way

before you get to actual pricing and negotiations. And often even your internal champion is clueless about this desire. Procurement doesn't want to do deals the last week of the quarter or the last week in December any more than you do.

Procurement departments have pipelines, revenue goals, and dashboards just like sales departments—with one exception: their pipelines and dashboards run in reverse.

We like to call this the Reverse Revenue Dashboard. Procurement staff are measured, and sometimes compensated, on how much money they save on each purchase. Just like us, they love to see their pipeline grow, and then see how much they can save.

Their dashboard may look something like this:

Company

Their Initial Price

Our Desired Price

Delta $

Delta %

Final

A few things to think about when considering the procurement mindset:

1 Their pipeline is *always* inbound.

2 The bigger their pipeline, the easier it is for them to actually negotiate harder with some clients than others.

3 They are often measured by percentages more than money. Which means even small percentages are a win for them.

4 They love to scare salespeople.

5 They rarely have the power to say "no" as much as they imply.

When negotiating, especially with procurement, you already have the advantage. It's just that nobody has ever taught you this until now. In fact, you are the house, the odds are stacked in your favor, and you are holding pocket aces.

Know your numbers and be sure to consider everyone's time on both sides of the table. It's not just about your time and your champions' time; it's about everyone this deal touches.

Here's a breakdown of how to track time spent for both sides.

Event	Vendor (Sales Rep)		Prospects (Buying Committees)	
	Internal People	Total Human Hours	Internal People	Total Human Hours
Live meetings	3	12	3	12
Your "debrief" of each conversation	3	5	6	8
Demos	4	12	7	12
Thinking about the deal	6	15	8	20
Talking to leadership teams separate of meeting debriefs	3	6	6	8
Spending time with others on your "deal team"	4	7	N/A	N/A
Getting advice from colleagues/references	2	4	3	3
Writing emails	1	15	1	15
Thinking about and responding to their emails	1	15	1	15
Grand Totals	**27**	**91**	**35**	**93**

For knowing your side's numbers—in this deal, how many people-hours has your organization put into:

1. Live meetings with your prospect
   - Initial call
   - Demo calls

2. Calls with your prospect

3. Your "debrief" of each conversation

4. Thinking about the deal, even on your commute

5. Talking to your leadership team separate of meeting debriefs

6. Spending time with others on your "deal team"

7. Getting advice from colleagues and coworkers

8. Writing emails

9. Thinking about and responding to their emails

For knowing their side's numbers—how many people-hours has their organization put into:

1. Live meetings with you
   - Initial call
   - Demo calls

2   Internal "take it back to the team" conversations

3   Thinking about the deal

4   Talking to their leadership team

5   Spending time with a competitor
    - Initial calls
    - Demo calls

6   Trialing vendors' products

7   Getting advice from colleagues and coworkers

8   All the emails, both internal and external

9   Thinking about and responding to your emails

Remember the following:

1   Include everyone's people-hours, not just yours.

2   For every thirty minutes you spend with your prospect, add another thirty for the "peripheral project time."

3   Don't forget to include everyone on your side.

4   For their side, include all their people at the meetings.

5 Also include all their people who are *not* at the meetings but they have to go and check with.

6 Also include what else their people could have been working on that did not happen because they were engaged in this process.
Example:

- You spend three hours in meetings with your prospect, from beginning to end.

  ○ There's a good chance you spend another three hours on the peripheral activities around this deal. That's six hours.

- You have two other people from your organization spending thirty minutes with this prospect.

  ○ Now, after that meeting you and your two coworkers probably spend another thirty minutes doing a debrief. That is an additional two-plus hours.

All in, you've spent approximately eight people-hours on this deal. And this doesn't include any opportunity costs associated with what did not get done and the impact that could have on your organization's revenue.

Now run the same exercise for the prospect's team.

- How many people on their side of the table showed up?

- How long was each meeting?

- How many people are on the relevant committee who never showed up to the meeting?

While it may be eight hours for your organization, it could be ten, twelve, or even fourteen hours for them. And again, this does not take into account any opportunity costs associated with this time.

Those fourteen hours are one of the aces you've been dealt.

And now you need to remember the dollarization exercises around Economic Impact from your discovery. This is the other ace you've been dealt.

You are now holding pocket aces.

Understanding their mindset, as we've covered above, is the flop. And the flop is showing ace, king, jack.

Now, let's roll out a conversation outline for working with procurement departments.

First you want to understand their role. Each company can be different. Here is a list of discovery questions to ask when you first speak with procurement. You should approach this as a Procurement Respect Contract and then ask these questions:

- Can you help me understand your role here?

- In addition to Commercial Terms, are you also the one who will help me go through the procurement process?

- What is important to you when working with a vendor?

- How long does the process take normally?

- What can I do to help you as we go through your process?

As they answer these questions, you may notice a change in their tone of voice. It may become slightly more relaxed. And you may come up with additional questions around the process or something else. Keep asking those questions. This is how you get procurement to fall in trust with you.

Now we move on to Commercial Terms. And you do the same thing you did with your champion.

"Our pricing is \$_____ . How does that feel?"

They will lie and say it's too much.

The good procurement people will stop after saying "too much" and expect you to lower the price. They will pause a very long time. Others will simply ask for a discount straight up.

Your only response is "OK, what are you expecting?"

The good procurement people will say "something less" or "something lower" and again expect you to offer a lower price. Don't fall for this. You would be discounting yourself, and you won't be done because they will reject this price too.

Your response is simply "Well, our pricing structure is based on what the market will bear." Now it's your turn to pause; count to at least "3 Mississippi Delta Queen" (you will do "3 Mississippi" way too fast).

You can now say, "What number are you thinking?" Because guess what, they have a number.

Your response is always simple. And frankly, it does not matter what their number is, because you are already prepared; they just want to feel heard.

Remember, they are now in a Child Ego state: they *want* a discount. It's our job to be a Nurturing Parent, and here is how we do that:

1 "There are four ways we can both leverage commercial terms, and each is worth 1.7 percentage points:

   • Marketing support in the form of case studies, logo usage, or a customer quote

   • Multiyear contracts

- Prepayment
- Additional licenses

Which of these can you commit to?"
Did you get distracted doing the math of 1.7 percent
× 4? So will they.

2 They will say something like, "That is not enough;
   we need it to be _____ or we cannot move forward." You respond simply, "I understand what you
   are asking, and this is our most favored pricing."
   (Yes, "most favored pricing" is a phrase they use.)

3 They will still ask for a bigger discount, and you
   revert to the most powerful negotiation statement
   ever used: "I understand; as I mentioned before,
   our pricing is based on what the market dictates.
   Why don't I do this—I will go back to [insert champion's name] and see if they have any ideas about
   where to find additional budget dollars."

In card-playing terms, this turn produced a jack. You
are now sitting on a full house and watching the others
make silly bets because they are bluffing.

You will then need to go back to your champion and
walk through the conversation with them and get their
advice. One of two things will happen: either they

will find the additional dollars, or they will say, "Ugh, I am not sure what to do; we may have to go to the competition."

Your response is where you can make use of those numbers you've tracked.

"Well, I am confused. When we spoke, you shared that the Economic Impact to your team is $_____. And from my math, it seems like your team put in thirty-plus people-hours to get us this far. Would you say that's accurate, or do you think it's been more than thirty hours?"

It kind of doesn't matter what their answer is.

These are the next questions to ask your champion:

1 "Well, I know you looked at the competitor, which is fair. I am curious:

- When we spoke, you mentioned we did these things better than the competition: _____, _____, and _____.

- And as I recall you said the difference in Economic Impact to your organization was _____.

- How much more time will it take you to go back and restart that conversation with the other vendor(s)?

- And about your legal team, how much time is it going to take them to review the new contract and go through redlines?

- And won't this additional time mean you miss your deadline? As I recall, you said if you didn't implement by [date] it's going to cause $_____ in Economic Impact."

2   "Now here is where I am confused:

- You've said we are $_____ better than the competition.

- You've said it's going to take _____ more hours for your team to rewind, review, and go through the process again.

- And you've said it's going to delay your rollout by _____, which you also say could have the Economic Impact of _____.

- And considering the delta between Commercial Terms is _____, are you sure you really want to walk away at this point?

- Well, considering the delta between our price and what is being asked is only $_____, and you've said it's going to take _____ hours compared to the _____ hours it's going to take to continue with someone else, are you sure that's the right decision?"

And the final hand produced the final ace. You've now converted your full house to quads, four aces.

The question is: are you willing to risk it?

Either you are sitting there going "Fuck yes! I am going to do this!" or you are thinking, "Great, Richard, that sounds awesome on paper, except I have goals to hit, pressure from my boss, a job to keep, bills to pay, and mouths to feed. So yeah, it all sounds wonderful, but I cannot take this risk."

I understand. I have been there myself, and yes, it's easier for someone like me who runs their own business to take these risks. But I too have mouths to feed. And I have no desire that anyone put their livelihood or families in a bad situation.

Our goal in sharing this strategy is to share best practices and not only give you the option to do this, but also give you a strong script to pull from. So often we are afraid to try things in sales because although we know what we want to do, we don't always have the right words. So often leaders tell us what we should do, but they have never done it themselves, and they don't have the right words either.

Now, for the sales leaders reading this section, if you want your team to do this, here are our suggestions:

1 You need to write the script.

2 You need to role-play it out loud a few times.

3 You need to be a leader and do it first.

4 You need to role-play with your team until it's perfect.

5 You need to stand up to your leadership team and let them know what you are going to do, and that they have three options:

- Do the discount and never say anything negative about you or your salesperson.

- Be willing to risk the deal, and if you lose, never say anything negative about you or your salesperson.

- Get on the phone and close it themselves, since they seem to be the expert.

9

Accountability Tactics

ONE OF THE BIGGEST challenges anyone in sales has is getting their prospects or customers to adhere to time-lines and complete specific tasks. Sometimes things cannot be helped. And yet there are things we can do to help make sure tasks are completed in a timely manner or at least prevent them from falling through the cracks.

Tactic 13: Assigning Accountability

Just as important as the pre-meeting email, Respect Contract, and good discovery is what happens right after a business conversation.

While lots of reps seem to have a post-meeting email they send, when we share ours with them, they tend to walk away incorporating much of it, if not all.

Here is an example of our post-meeting email. In this context it is the email sent after a first meeting has occurred. Of course, find a template that works for you; we recommend you send something like this after every meeting. Below we will walk you through exactly why ours is written this way.

Subject Line: Prospect's Company/Seller's Company: Next Step/Call Notes/Resources/Commercial Terms

Hey, Sarah and Bob,

Great speaking with you today. I'd like you to please use this email as a summary of our conversation. Please respond and let me know if I captured everything correctly.

Thanks,
Richard

You can grab my time on the calendar by
CLICKING HERE

Next Steps

- Richard to include a link to the syllabus <u>CLICK HERE</u>

- Richard to include a link to the online training portal <u>CLICK HERE</u>

- Richard to include a link to G2 Crowd Customer Reviews <u>CLICK HERE</u>

- Sarah and Bob to determine whether additional conversations with Richard and some other team members are worthwhile at this point

- Richard to make contact again around Feb 1 if he doesn't hear back sooner

Challenges & Training

- Working on developing a sales methodology
  - Up-level the skills
  - Challenger, Spin
  - Bob familiar with MEDDIC

At the end of the engagement, we expect the team to be better at _____, _____, and _____.

- Having a common language

- Discovery—Customer Profile
  - No understanding how to do customer discovery

- ◦ Go to quoting too quickly
- ◦ Objections
- ◦ Negotiation for Pricing
  - Multiyear contracts
  - Long-term relationships
- Bob
  - ◦ Qualification
  - ◦ Spend time on opportunities that are not worth the time
- Accountability
  - ◦ AE's are not owning a book of business
  - ◦ AE's cannot easily answer "where are we in the deal?"
- Want to help managers better manage reps to pipeline and actually manage people
- Set up the skills now to be able to be more consultative during their sales conversations

Sales Team Structure

- SDRS—45
- AES—65
- 4 Sales Leaders Outside Reps

Sales Process Overview & Notes

- Avg Sales Cycle—29 days
- Avg Sale Price—$5,000-$7,000
- Win rate—
  - 14% on net new customers
  - 80%-85% on existing customers
- Inbound vs. Outbound Quantity

Timeline

- What is the line in the sand?
- What happens if you do not meet this deadline?

Additional Resources

- The Evolution of Sales—Welcome to N.E.A.T. Selling
- 6 Things Every Technical Mind Should Know About the Sales Process
- 5 Tips When Hiring a Sales Consultant

Commercial Terms

- $37,500/year
  - Qualification
- 7.3% Pre-Pay Discount for 2 years

What to Notice and Why It Works

Each part of this email is written in a specific way.

1 **Subject Line: Company Name/THCG Next Steps/Call Notes/Additional Resources/Commercial Terms**

- Easily identifiable in someone's inbox.

- Specific to the contents of the email and the fact you just had a conversation.

- The subject line makes it easy to determine whether the email should be circulated.

- All additional emails with this prospect and customer are on this thread, so again it's easy to identify; no more hunting around through five emails with your prospect or customer.

- Use of Commercial Terms in subject line is consistent with the conversations and reinforces the phrase. Which reinforces that we are not a commodity and that there is an exchange of money for goods and services that is fair and equal to all parties.

2 **First Paragraph**
- Short, simple and to the point.
- Accountability is assigned by asking them to respond and confirm everything is correct.

Now they have a responsibility to respond and confirm. (Technically, sure it's on me. I like to think if anything goes wrong, I am 51 percent to blame, they are 49 percent.)

3 Signature
- Purposely after the first two sentences. In case they want my contact information, it's right there. Also, most emails are read on a phone, so I want the message to be short so that they actually read it. Once they start reading, they cannot stop.

4 Next Steps
- Purposely near the top. If read on a cell phone, it's seen sooner and drives urgency.
- Assigns responsibilities to all parties.
- Next steps are listed clearly using bullet points.

5 Challenges
- This is where we prove Active Listening.
- Always get specific about their pains.
- Always get specific about their Economic Impact.

6 Organizational Structure (Not always a part of the email)
- This can be whatever you want it to be.
- Often helps identify other parts of the decision-making process.

7   **Timeline**
- Want to implement by [date].
- Lack of implementation has an Economic Impact of _____.

8   **Additional Resources**
   (Not always a part of the email)
- If you have them, it's OK to send them.

9   **Commercial Terms**
- Ties back to the subject line if Commercial Terms were discussed.
- Specifically at the bottom of the email to encourage them to read it.

Here are the typical questions I get when I teach this approach.

1   **Question: Wow, this email looks really long, Richard, should we shorten it?**
   My response is simple: "I don't care." This is as much for me as it is for them. And when I train teams, it's one of the most requested and executed ideas the teams use. (And to be honest, the hippie lettuce didn't really help my memory.)

2   **Question: Do you type this when on the call or do you take notes and then write it?**

Answer:

- Actually, it's a complete template. Even the first few bullet points of each section are there, so all I have to do is type the notes. The template helps me stay true to my sales process and ensure everything is included.

- Remember, it's about the Buyer's Experience. This enhances that experience.

- As part of my Respect Contract, I state the following and point accordingly to my camera, screen and laptop: "Hey, _____ , so you know, my camera is here, you are over on another screen, and if you see me looking down and typing, I am just taking notes and I will email them to you after this call. I don't want you to think I am on Facebook or LinkedIn." While everyone knows this is probably what's happening, I want them to know for sure. And I want them to know that if they get distracted, I will be able to tell.

3 **Question: Why are Commercial Terms at the end?**
Because Commercial Terms is in the subject line, we know they are going to go and look for it. By placing it at the bottom, it means they have to at least scroll through the whole email.

Writing effective emails is one of the easiest things for a salesperson to implement. It will also make you stand out among all the salespeople your prospects and customers speak with. And we don't mean just your competitors—all salespeople.

Now, you won't win every deal with this tactic. But they will remember you long after you're gone, and that leaves a door open for a future engagement.

In fact, when I lose deals, I often use this email template to reconnect six months or a year later to see if they are happy with their decision. They remember this template, it's familiar, and because of the subject line, the open rate is high as well as the response rate.

10

The Never-Ending Journey

NOW YOU'RE READY TO go on your Seller's Journey.

You have your compass.

You have your map.

You have your tactics.

You have your wisdom.

You have your respect.

You have your way to assign accountability.

While you have reached the end of this book, your Seller's Journey has just begun—and it never ends. And the world is ever changing, so we encourage you to keep learning, keep a growth mindset. Try to love your failures. Try to embrace your wins. Support others who you feel could use some help on their journey.

You've earned the right to be as successful as you want to be in this career or any other you choose.

From the bottom of my heart, thank you for going on this journey along with me. You are appreciated in ways you may not even understand. And yes, you can still call or email me if you want your money back.

Richard

Epilogue: OK, so now what?

Wait! Don't go yet!

(This is like the movie scene that happens after the credits roll.)

The question I get most often after sales training or I give some advice is "So what's the best way to implement this stuff, Richard?"

My first answer is usually something like, "Well, which of these things do you already kind of do, but if you started to focus on them you could do better?" And they will pick a tactic or two, and I'll say, "Great, start there, and only focus on that one thing for an entire week."

That doesn't mean they (or you) cannot do something else; it simply means you are going to actively and intently pursue one thing, and one thing only.

Like many things in life, as much as we want to do it all (that Child Ego again), it's simply not that easy. Serena Williams didn't try to work on every part of her tennis game each time she practiced. She focused on one part at a time: her forehand, her serve, etc. And that means for the whole session. A golfer doesn't get better at putting by simply putting for ten minutes, and then hitting out of the sand for ten minutes, and then hitting a driver for ten minutes. We get better by focusing with intent on practicing a single thing at a time. Eventually, one thing will get to the next, and then eventually several may blend together. However, that is not where we start.

We start at the beginning. We start with one thing.

If you don't know where to start, our suggestion is to start with the Respect Contracts. All other strategies and tactics taught here flow from there.

Enjoy your journey!

Wait, one more thing...

It's either a shameless plug or you can send me a "nast-e-mail" and ask for your money back. Want me to come and train your team? Email me: richard@rharris415.com.

Acknowledgments

IN ADDITION TO MY wife and sons, there are so many people I need to acknowledge from my entire life. Hopefully I do not miss any of you. You have each influenced me somewhere in my life and for this I am truly grateful and love you all.

Mom, Dad, Lynn, Machya, Joyce, Grammie, Papa, Meme, Jeff, John S, Julianne, Uncle John, Aunt Sara, Ethan, Catherine, Pam, Martha Kate, Aunt Patsy, Uncle EJ, Jennifer, Graham, Ned, Allison, David, Molly, BA, Butch, Riff, Fresh, Lish, Doba, Shnuff, PCP, Eddie, Poofoo, Kelsey, Kenny, Scott T, Troy, Dickie, George, Janet, Noel, Maura, Oscar, Kim, Ann, Pauline, Roque, Nick, Jeff, Tim, Alan, KD, KG, John, and Scott L.

About the Author

RICHARD HARRIS is an award-winning and globally recognized sales trainer and GTM strategist. As the founder of the Harris Consulting Group and the N.E.A.T. Selling philosophy, methodology, and process, he has dedicated over twenty years to the world of sales, having held roles from sales development representative to vice-president of sales, and everything in between. Richard works with Fortune 500 companies as well as startups, and his clients include Zoom, Salesforce, Pager Duty, Human Interest, Dusty Robotics, and Gainsight, among others. He lives in northern California with his wife, Cathy; sons, Riley and Bodhi; and two Cavapoos, Lola and Luna.

Thanks for reading
The Seller's Journey.
Let's connect!

VISIT MY SITE:
theharrisconsultinggroup.com

**SCHEDULE A VIDEO MEETING WITH ME FOR
AN INTRODUCTION OR COACHING SESSION:**
theharrisconsultinggroup.com/contact-us

FIND ME ON SOCIAL MEDIA:

f facebook.com/harrisconsultingllc

instagram.com/rharris415

X twitter.com/rharris415

in linkedin.com/in/rharris415

youtube.com/@sales.training.rharris

If you enjoyed this book and its message, please
consider offering your review on your preferred
online retailer's website or online forum.

This book is also available as an ebook.

Made in the USA
Las Vegas, NV
19 August 2024